THE FUNDAMENTALS
OF
SPECIAL EDUCATION

A PRACTICAL APPROACH TO SPECIAL EDUCATION FOR EVERY TEACHER

The Fundamentals of Special Education
A Practical Guide for Every Teacher

The Legal Foundations of Special Education
A Practical Guide for Every Teacher

Effective Assessment for Students With Special Needs
A Practical Guide for Every Teacher

Effective Instruction for Students With Special Needs
A Practical Guide for Every Teacher

*Working With Families and Community Agencies
to Support Students With Special Needs*
A Practical Guide for Every Teacher

Public Policy, School Reform, and Special Education
A Practical Guide for Every Teacher

Teaching Students With Sensory Disabilities
A Practical Guide for Every Teacher

Teaching Students With Medical, Physical, and Multiple Disabilities
A Practical Guide for Every Teacher

Teaching Students With Learning Disabilities
A Practical Guide for Every Teacher

Teaching Students With Communication Disorders
A Practical Guide for Every Teacher

Teaching Students With Emotional Disturbance
A Practical Guide for Every Teacher

Teaching Students With Mental Retardation
A Practical Guide for Every Teacher

Teaching Students With Gifts and Talents
A Practical Guide for Every Teacher

The
FUNDAMENTALS
OF
SPECIAL EDUCATION

A Practical Guide for Every Teacher

BOB ALGOZZINE
JIM YSSELDYKE

CORWIN PRESS
A SAGE Publications Company
Thousand Oaks, California

For information:

Corwin Press
A Sage Publications Company
2455 Teller Road
Thousand Oaks, California 91320
www.corwinpress.com

Sage Publications Ltd.
1 Oliver's Yard
55 City Road
London EC1Y 1SP
United Kingdom

Sage Publications India Pvt. Ltd.
B-42, Panchsheel Enclave
Post Box 4109
New Delhi 110 017 India

Printed in the United States of America

Library of Congress Cataloging-in-Publication Data

Algozzine, Robert.
The fundamentals of special education: A practical guide for every teacher/
Bob Algozzine, James E. Ysseldyke.
    p. cm.
Includes bibliographical references and index.
ISBN 1-4129-3941-0 (cloth)
ISBN 1-4129-3894-5 (pbk.)
    1. Special education—United States. 2. Exceptional children—United States.
3. Exceptional children—Services for—United States. 4. Special education
teachers—Training of—United States. I. Ysseldyke, James E. II. Title.
LC3981.A663 2006
371.9—dc22

                                                              2005037817

This book is printed on acid-free paper.

06 07 08 09 10 9 8 7 6 5 4 3 2 1

Acquisitions Editor:	Kylee M. Liegl
Editorial Assistant:	Nadia Kashper
Production Editor:	Denise Santoyo
Copy Editor:	Marilyn Power Scott
Typesetter:	C&M Digitals (P) Ltd.
Indexer:	Kathy Paparchontis
Cover Designer:	Michael Dubowe

Contents

About *A Practical Approach to Special*
   Education for Every Teacher   vii
   Acknowledgments   viii

About the Authors   xi

Self-Assessment 1   1

Introduction to *The Fundamentals of Special Education*   5

1. What Is Special Education?   9

2. Why Do We Have Special Education?   11
   The Evolution of Special Education   11
   Special Education Today   12
   Protection Against Discrimination   13

3. Who Receives Special Education?   15
   Special Education's Categories   15

4. How Many Students Receive Special Education?   19
   Steady Growth   19
      Reasons for Growth   20
   The Continuing Demand for Special Educators   20

5. How Are Students Identified
   for Special Education Services?   21
   Accommodating Students With Exceptionalities
      in General Education Classrooms   21
   The Special Education Process   22
      Determining Eligibility   22
      Delivering Special Instruction   22
      Evaluating Progress   24

6. **What Services Do Special Education Students Receive?** 25
   Direct Services 25
   Indirect Services 26
   Related Services 26

7. **Where Are Students Taught?** 27
   Least Restrictive Environment 27

8. **How Does Diversity Influence Special Education?** 29
   Diverse Students 29
     Dropping Out 30
     Drop-Out Rates of Students With Special Needs 31
   Diverse Educational Settings 31
   Variations by State 32

9. **What About Students Who Are Gifted and Talented?** 33
   Intellectual Ability 34
   Creative Ability 34
   Specific Academic Ability 34
   Leadership Ability 35
   Ability in the Visual and Performing Arts 35
   Identifying Gifts and Talents 35

10. **Special Education in Perspective** 37

11. **What Have We Learned?** 39
    Key Points 39
    Key Vocabulary 40

Self-Assessment 2 45

Answer Key for Self-Assessments 49

On Your Own 51

Resources 53
   Books 53
   Journals and Articles 54
   Organizations 55

References 57

Index 59

About
A Practical Approach to Special Education for Every Teacher

S pecial education means specially designed instruction for students with unique learning needs. Students receive special education for many reasons. Students with disabilities such as mental retardation, hearing impairments (including deafness), speech or language impairments, visual impairments (including blindness), emotional disturbance, orthopedic impairments, autism, traumatic brain injury, other health impairments, or specific learning disabilities are entitled to special education services. Students who are gifted and talented also receive special education. Special education services are delivered in many settings, including regular classes, resource rooms, and separate classes. The 13 books of this collection will help you teach students with disabilities and those with gifts and talents. Each book focuses on a specific area of special education and can be used individually or in conjunction with all or some of the other books. Six of the books provide the background and content knowledge you need in order to work effectively with all students with unique learning needs:

Book 1: The Fundamentals of Special Education

Book 2: The Legal Foundations of Special Education

Book 3: Effective Assessment for Students With Special Needs

Book 4: Effective Instruction for Students With Special Needs

Book 5: Working With Families and Community Agencies to Support Students With Special Needs

Book 6: Public Policy, School Reform, and Special Education

Seven of the books focus on teaching specific groups of students who receive special education:

Book 7:   Teaching Students With Sensory Disabilities

Book 8:   Teaching Students With Medical, Physical, and Multiple Disabilities

Book 9:   Teaching Students With Learning Disabilities

Book 10: Teaching Students With Communication Disorders

Book 11: Teaching Students With Emotional Disturbance

Book 12: Teaching Students With Mental Retardation

Book 13: Teaching Students With Gifts and Talents

All of the books in *A Practical Approach to Special Education for Every Teacher* will help you to make a difference in the lives of all students, especially those with unique learning needs.

ACKNOWLEDGMENTS

The approach we take in *A Practical Approach to Special Education for Every Teacher* is an effort to change how professionals learn about special education. The 13 separate books are a result of prodding from our students and from professionals in the field to provide a set of materials that "cut to the chase" in teaching them about students with disabilities and about building the capacity of systems to meet those students' needs. Teachers told us that in their classes they always confront students with special learning needs and students their school district has assigned a label to (e.g., students with learning disabilities). Our students and the professionals we worked with wanted a very practical set of texts that gave them the necessary **information** *about* **the students** (e.g., federal definitions, student characteristics) and specific **information on** *what to do about* **the students** (assessment and teaching strategies, approaches that work). They also wanted the opportunity to purchase parts of textbooks, rather than entire texts, to learn what they needed.

The production of this collection would not have been possible without the support and assistance of many colleagues. Professionals associated with Corwin Press—Faye Zucker, Kylee Liegl, Robb Clouse—helped us work through the idea of introducing special education differently, and their support in helping us do it is deeply appreciated.

Faye Ysseldyke and Kate Algozzine, our children, and our grandchildren also deserve recognition. They have made the problems associated with the project very easy to diminish, deal with, or dismiss. Every day in every way, they enrich our lives and make us better. We are grateful for them.

About the Authors

Bob Algozzine, PhD, is professor in the Department of Educational Leadership at the University of North Carolina at Charlotte and project codirector of the U.S. Department of Education–supported Behavior and Reading Improvement Center. With 25 years of research experience and extensive firsthand knowledge of teaching students classified as seriously emotionally disturbed (and other equally useless terms), Algozzine is a uniquely qualified staff developer, conference speaker, and teacher of behavior management and effective teaching courses.

As an active partner and collaborator with professionals in the Charlotte-Mecklenburg schools in North Carolina and as an editor of several journals focused on special education, Algozzine keeps his finger on the pulse of current special education practice. He has written more than 250 manuscripts on special education topics, authoring many popular books and textbooks on how to manage emotional and social behavior problems. Through *A Practical Approach to Special Education for Every Teacher,* Algozzine hopes to continue to help improve the lives of students with special needs—and the professionals who teach them.

Jim Ysseldyke, PhD, is Birkmaier Professor in the Department of Educational Psychology, director of the School Psychology Program, and director of the Center for Reading Research at the University of Minnesota. Widely requested as a staff developer and conference speaker, he brings more than 30 years of research and teaching experience to educational professionals around the globe.

As the former director of the federally funded National Center on Educational Outcomes, Ysseldyke conducted research and provided technical support that helped to boost the academic performance of students with disabilities and improve school assessment techniques nationally. Today he continues to work to improve the education of students with disabilities.

The author of more than 300 publications on special education and school psychology, Ysseldyke is best known for his textbooks on assessment, effective instruction, issues in special education, and other cutting-edge areas of education and school psychology. With *A Practical Approach to Special Education for Every Teacher*, he seeks to equip educators with practical knowledge and methods that will help them to better engage students in exploring—and meeting—all their potentials.

Self-Assessment 1

Before you begin this book, check your knowledge of the content being covered. Choose the best answer for each of the following questions.

1. The educational system that is an alternative to the general education system is

   a. Special education

   b. Gifted and talented education

   c. Compulsory education

   d. Separated education

2. The year 2000 marked the _____ anniversary of federal legislation mandating a free, appropriate public education for individuals with disabilities.

   a. 10th

   b. 25th

   c. 50th

   d. 100th

3. Federal law does not require states to provide special education to

   a. Students with emotional problems

   b. Students who are over the age of 21

   c. Students who are in preschool

   d. Students who are in high school

4. Special education services are provided to approximately
   _____ students each year.

   a. 2 million

   b. 4 million

   c. 6 million

   d. 8 million

5. Federal laws were passed to protect the rights of individuals with disabilities because

   a. They were not being treated the same as their peers without disabilities.

   b. They were performing below expectations when compared to their peers without disabilities.

   c. They were entitled to special services by laws written in the 1800s but forgotten in recent times.

   d. They were entitled to special services by state laws governing education.

6. To receive special education, a child must be declared eligible for services in at least one of _____ categories accepted by the federal government and most states.

   a. 3

   b. 5

   c. 11

   d. 13

7. The process of requesting information to decide if a student is eligible for special education services is called

   _____.

   a. Referral

   b. Examination

c. Opportunity to learn

d. Intervention

8. Direct, indirect, and related are all

    a. Types of general education interventions

    b. Types of special education services

    c. Types of counseling for students who are gifted and talented

    d. Prereferral interventions

9. The guiding principle of special education that directs that students should be educated in environments as much like general education as possible is known as

    a. Inclusive education

    b. Opportunity to learn

    c. Least restrictive environment

    d. Educational due process

10. The prevailing belief about special education today is that

    a. All students are more alike than they are different.

    b. All students need special education at some time in their lives.

    c. Special education should be provided in self-contained classrooms for most children requiring special education services.

    d. Special education services should be available to more children than are currently being served.

REFLECTION

After you answer the multiple-choice questions, think about how you would answer the following questions:

- What is special education and whom does it serve?
- What does IDEA mandate?
- What is inclusion and what does it mean for teachers?

Introduction to
The Fundamentals
of Special Education

Terry was a living legend at Magnolia Middle School. Everybody wondered what Terry would do next. Constantly asking questions, teasing other students, telling jokes, and generally disrupting the class were Terry's trademarks.

Whatever the level or kind of work her teacher assigns, **Donnelle** demonstrates superior academic performance. She works diligently on everything, sometimes redoing an assignment after the final grade has been recorded. Most of her classmates look to Donnelle for academic, athletic, social, and emotional leadership during the school day. Teachers like teaching Donnelle because she keeps them actively involved in their content areas.

Antoinette does not see well, but she is doing quite well in her classes at Jamestown High School with the assistance of her teachers. She has a warm personality and outstanding knowledge of science and mathematics. Dr. Roberson, the principal of the school, is legally blind and has encouraged Antoinette to attend his alma mater, Kansas State University.

(Continued)

(Continued)

> **Ann** is 20 years old and has been receiving special education services since elementary school. These services have helped her learn to function independently and make adjustments for her mental retardation. This year she is finishing high school. She and her family are asking important questions about what her life will be like without the support provided by special education staff. As Ann makes the transition from working and learning in school to living and working in the community, she will manage her new challenges just like the friends who will be graduating with her: courageously.

E very school has students like Terry, Donnelle, Antoinette, and Ann. These students are known for what they do, and what they do sometimes conflicts with what teachers and others believe they should do. Sometimes their disabilities interfere with their progress in school. Special education programs address problems and assist people with disabilities.

Most students—whatever their special needs—can be taught in the same classrooms as their neighbors and peers. If you teach in a general education classroom, you will probably teach students with disabilities. Providing special assistance to students who need it is one of the reasons that people become teachers.

Just like general education teachers, special education teachers have full days. Special education teachers may teach basic skills classes to help students learn to read, write, and do math better. They may teach learning strategies classes to help students develop skills they need for academics. They may also have classes of students who have social and emotional problems.

Special education teachers face the same concerns about their students as do other teachers. All students worry about what their friends think about them, their social lives, and their futures. A general education teacher deals with these concerns but may also be concerned that students accept those who have special needs. General education teachers want to ensure that exceptional students are integrated into their general education classes and that all students develop the basic skills they need to succeed. Even though general education and special education classrooms are different settings, the types of students in them and the ways in which subjects are taught are similar. For example, both special and general education teachers structure their teaching to accommodate students' individual needs. All effective teachers do this. They use information from tests and classroom observations to plan instruction and to evaluate the effects of that instruction. And special and general education teachers both have to maintain orderly classrooms that support learning for all of their students.

There was a time when students of all ages and capabilities were educated in a single classroom. In many communities, the one-room schoolhouse disappeared because it became more and more difficult for a single teacher to meet the diverse needs of a large number of students. Educators believed that grouping students by age and by subject matter would make their teaching more effective. A by-product of this thinking was separate classes for students with special needs. This parallel system of general and special education continues today.

1

What Is Special Education?

Education is the process of learning and changing as a result of schooling and other experiences. **Special education** is instruction designed for students with special learning needs. Some students with special needs have difficulty learning in general classrooms; they need special education to function in school. Others do well in general classrooms; they need special education to help master additional skills and reach their full potential in school. Special education is evidence of society's willingness to recognize and respond to the individual needs of students and to support the needs of general school programs to accommodate those needs.

2

Why Do We Have Special Education?

The year 2000 marked the 25th anniversary of federal legislation mandating a free, appropriate public education for individuals with disabilities. During 2000, more than 6 million people from birth to age 21 received some form of special education (ERIC Clearinghouse on Disabilities and Gifted Education, 2001; U.S. Department of Education, 2000, 2001, 2002). These people are being taught by specially trained teachers in a variety of instructional environments that are designed to meet their unique learning needs.

THE EVOLUTION OF SPECIAL EDUCATION

Compulsory school attendance began in the United States around 1850. By 1916, all children in every state were required to attend school. Although requiring students to go to school was probably a good idea, making it happen was not easy. For one thing, many families were not convinced that school was the best place to receive an education. (Even today, many families choose to educate their children at home.) Another issue was deciding what to do with students once they were in school. The class-graded system that exists today was one solution to the problem of structuring the school day. Early educators reasoned that students should be taught specific content and that the content could best be organized into graded units.

Students with special learning needs always have been and always will be a part of the educational system. But before they were required to attend school, they did not attract much attention. Progressive social policy brought students with exceptionalities to school. Traditional graded units failed as the best place to transmit content to these students, and teachers and other school personnel argued that the presence of exceptional students not only interfered with the training of others but also hindered the education of the exceptional students themselves. In response, physicians and early special educators developed a formal alternative to the general education system: special education.

Early public education offered two choices: Students were taught in a lockstep, graded class or in an ungraded special class. Educators of the time often treated special education classes as clearinghouses for students who would ultimately be going to institutions for physical, mental, or moral "deviance."

SPECIAL EDUCATION TODAY

Today, students with special needs are no longer thought of as deviants or locked away. Special education now offers a sophisticated series of educational alternatives for them. In 1975, President Gerald Ford signed the Education for All Handicapped Children Act (Public Law 94–142)—the first compulsory special education law (now known as the Individuals With Disabilities Education Improvement Act, or IDEA). This law guarantees students with disabilities and their parents certain rights, and it places specific responsibilities on people who organize and deliver special education services. In brief, the law mandates the following:

A free, appropriate public education for children with disabilities

Well-planned school programs tailored to meet students' unique learning needs (**individualized education programs, or IEPs**)

Protection of the rights of students with disabilities under the same legal provisions that protect the rights of students without disabilities (**due process**)

The right of students with disabilities to have decisions made about them in an unbiased manner (**protection in evaluation procedures**, or PEP)

Educational environments like those provided students without disabilities (**least restrictive environment**, or LRE)

PROTECTION AGAINST DISCRIMINATION

Public Law 94–142 was passed to protect the rights of students with disabilities because they were not being treated the same way as their peers without disabilities. The law guarantees to students with disabilities and their families the rights that other students have long enjoyed; it protects them from educational policies that discriminate against people with disabilities.

There was a time when placement in a special education class meant the end of a student's normal educational and social experiences. Students were placed in special classes on the recommendation of one teacher or on the basis of their performances on one test. Once assigned to special classes, students often remained in those classes for the remainder of their schooling. This system produced special class enrollments in which students of color were overrepresented; this problem persists (National Research Council, 2002; President's Commission on Excellence in Special Education, 2002). There were also problems with the programs themselves. Some institutions and special schools substituted harsh discipline for the educational services that students with exceptionalities needed. Parents and professionals argued that these practices did not reflect sound educational policy or equality of opportunity and lobbied for laws that mandated change. Their legacy is the system of special education that exists today, in which the rights of students with exceptionalities are recognized.

3

Who Receives Special Education?

Exceptional students are those who have disabilities or extraordinary gifts and talents. These students differ from their peers in the ways they perform tasks used to measure school achievement. The similarities between exceptional students and their peers far exceed the differences. However, some of the differences are central to success in school. These differences are of concern to teachers, parents, and the students themselves.

SPECIAL EDUCATION'S CATEGORIES

Today, most states organize their special education departments along categorical lines. A **category** is simply a name assigned to a group of exceptional students. Although the names of the categories vary slightly from state to state, special education generally is provided to students within the following categories (U.S. Department of Education, 2002):

1. **Autism:** Students with autism have special learning needs in areas related to verbal and nonverbal communication and social interaction. Symptoms of autism are generally evident before age 3 and adversely affect

educational performance. Less than 1 percent of the school-aged population is classified in this category.

2. **Blindness or Visual Impairment**: Students in this category have special learning needs in areas requiring functional use of vision. Less than 1 percent of the school-aged population is classified in this category.

3. **Deafness and Blindness:** Students in this category have special learning needs in areas requiring functional use of hearing *and* vision. Less than 1 percent of the school-aged population is classified in this category.

4. **Deafness or Hearing Impairment:** Students in this category have special learning needs in areas requiring functional use of hearing. Less than 1 percent of the school-aged population is classified in this category.

5. **Emotional Disturbance**: Students with emotional disturbance have special learning needs in areas requiring functional use of social and emotional skills. About 1 percent of the school-aged population is classified in this category.

6. **Gifted and Talented**: Students in this category have special learning needs in areas requiring functional use of intelligence and artistic ability. About 3 percent of the school-aged population is classified in this category.

7. **Mental Retardation**: Students with mental retardation have special learning needs in areas requiring functional use of intelligence and adaptive behavior. About 1 percent of the school-aged population is classified in this category.

8. **Multiple or Severe Disabilities**: Students in this category have special learning needs in more than one area requiring functional use of skills. Less than 1 percent of the school-aged population is classified in this category.

9. **Orthopedic or Other Health Impairments:** Students in this category have special learning needs in areas requiring functional use of hands, arms, legs, feet, and other body parts. Less than 1 percent of the school-aged population is classified in this category.

10. **Specific Learning Disabilities**: Students with learning disabilities have special learning needs in areas requiring functional use of listening, speaking, reading, writing, reasoning, and arithmetic skills. About 5 percent of the school-aged population is classified in this category.

11. **Speech or Language Impairments:** Students in this category have special learning needs in areas requiring functional use of language and communication skills. About 3 percent of the school-aged population is classified in this category.

12. **Traumatic Brain Injury:** Students in this category have special learning needs in areas related to injuries to the brain that result in total or partial loss of ability or psychosocial adjustment. The injuries adversely affect their educational performance. This category does not include brain injuries that are congenital or degenerative or brain injuries induced by birth trauma. Less than 1 percent of the school-aged population is classified in this category.

In some states, each category of students has one consultant or supervisor. In these states, school districts usually organize their special education programs along categorical lines. Other states have a single administrator who is responsible for several or all categories of exceptional students. In these states, services may be delivered in cross-categorical rather than categorical programs.

4

How Many Students Receive Special Education?

More than six million infants, toddlers, children, and young adults receive special education services in school or community settings in the United States every year (U.S. Department of Education, 2001, 2002). That number is roughly equivalent to the number of full-time undergraduates in four-year colleges and universities. It is also about the same as the combined populations of Idaho, Montana, Nevada, North Dakota, South Dakota, and Wyoming and exceeds the population of each of 32 of the 50 states.

STEADY GROWTH

According to the U.S. Department of Education (2002), the number of children with disabilities receiving special education and related services has steadily grown since passage of the Education for All Handicapped Children Act in 1975. The number of students aged 6–21 years receiving special education reached 5,775,722 in 2000–2001, about a 3 percent increase over the previous year. During the 1990s, the number of students served grew 30.3 percent (about 3 percent a year), from 4,253,018 in 1989–90 to

5,541,166 in 1998–99. The growth in the number of children with disabilities exceeded the growth in both the resident population and school enrollment. For this same period, growth in the United States' resident population of children aged 6–21 years was 9.7 percent (from 56,688,000 to 62,204,713). School enrollment grew 14.1 percent, from 40,608,342 to 46,349,803.

Reasons for Growth

The source of this growth is generally attributed to increases in students classified with learning disabilities. Reasons for growth in this category include a desire not to stigmatize students with other labels, the need created by legal actions to reclassify students previously categorized as mentally retarded, and the desire to obtain supplemental instruction for students in need when other compensatory education programs become less available.

THE CONTINUING DEMAND
FOR SPECIAL EDUCATORS

About 340,000 teachers and 460,000 related-services personnel provide special education services (U.S. Department of Education, 2000). The growing number of students in special education programs means that new special education positions continue to be created, and shortages of special educators are chronic. The growth in enrollment has also created problems for school personnel who have to decide how to pay for expanding programs. The costs of educating students with special needs sometimes compete with the costs of educating students in general education programs. The high rate of identification of some groups of children with disabilities (e.g., specific learning disabilities, speech and language impairments) creates great need for a large, highly qualified pool of special education teachers and specialists (e.g., speech-language pathologists) to meet their needs (U. S. Department of Education, 2002).

5

How Are Students Identified for Special Education Services?

Special education is a service delivery system. Students who need special education must be declared eligible for its services before those services can be provided in public school programs. This is different from the way it works in general education, where students are provided an education between the ages specified in each state's laws.

ACCOMMODATING STUDENTS WITH EXCEPTIONALITIES IN GENERAL EDUCATION CLASSROOMS

Some students with exceptionalities are identified before they enter school. Others are identified after they start school, as their difficulties or outstanding progress make their special needs clear. Special education programs today emphasize **inclusion**: educating students with exceptionalities in general education classrooms. This means that general education teachers must try to accommodate students with special needs in their classes.

Only if these students cannot be accommodated are they placed in special classes.

THE SPECIAL EDUCATION PROCESS

The process of requesting information to decide if a student is eligible for special education services is called **referral**. Finding ways to keep exceptional students in general education classrooms is called **prereferral intervention**. If a prereferral intervention does not help the student, the formal special education process begins. Picture a three-stage progression:

1. Determining eligibility

2. Delivering special instruction

3. Evaluating progress

Determining Eligibility

The first stage, determining eligibility, begins when students progress unusually quickly or slowly at home or at school. In some situations, a general education teacher may find that a student does not learn without special help. A team of professionals then gathers information and uses it to decide whether a student is eligible for special services. A key factor in eligibility is the *extent* to which the student does not perform like others. For example, problems related to physical performance (e.g., not seeing, hearing, moving as well as peers) are the basis for assigning students to several of the categories of exceptionality.

Delivering Special Instruction

In the second stage of the process, delivering special instruction, the student receives individualized services from trained professionals. Once a team of professionals has decided that a student is eligible for special education and will profit from specially designed instruction and the student's family gives its consent, service delivery begins. What happens next varies with the nature of the individual's special needs. During this phase, a formal document is written: the **individualized education program (IEP)**. The student's IEP serves as a guide for instruction delivery. The IEP describes in writing:

1. The student's present levels of educational performance, including how the specific disability affects the student's involvement and progress in the general curriculum or (for preschool children) how the disability affects participation in appropriate activities

2. Measurable annual goals (including benchmarks or short-term objectives) that enable the student to progress in the general curriculum and meet the other educational needs that result from the student's disability

3. The special education and related services to be provided to the student and the program modifications or supports for school personnel that will be provided in order to attain the annual goals

4. The extent, if any, to which the student will not participate with peers without disabilities in general education classes

5. Individual modifications in the administration of statewide or districtwide assessments of student achievement or—if the IEP team determines that the student will not participate in a particular achievement assessment—a statement of why the assessment is not appropriate and how the student will be assessed

6. The projected date for beginning services and the anticipated frequency, location, and duration of those services

7. Beginning at age 14 and updated annually, a statement of the transition service needs of the student (such as participation in advanced-placement courses or a vocational education program)

8. Beginning at age 16 (or younger, if determined appropriate by the IEP team), a statement of needed transition services, including interagency responsibilities or any needed linkages

9. Beginning at least one year before the student reaches the age of majority under state law, a statement that the student has been informed of the rights under this title that will transfer to the student on reaching the age of majority

10. How progress toward the annual goals will be measured

11. How the student's family will be regularly informed of progress toward annual goals (at least as often as parents of students without disabilities are informed of progress) and the extent to which that progress is sufficient to achieve the goals by the end of the year

Evaluating Progress

The third stage of the special education process is evaluating progress. A student's progress is monitored to determine the need for continuing, changing, or concluding special services. A student with a disability must be evaluated at least once a year. Every three years, a formal reevaluation is necessary to determine if a student is still eligible for special services. Students can be removed from special programs any time they have shown sufficient progress.

General education classroom teachers play an important role in the special education process. They often are the first to notice that a student's performance is different from that of other class members. They gather information and try alternative teaching techniques (prereferral intervention). They also collect the information that is used to decide whether a student is eligible for special education services. General classroom teachers are part of the team that makes the decision about how to educate a student who is exceptional. They also are involved in student progress evaluations and program evaluations.

6

What Services Do Special Education Students Receive?

S pecial education is a complex system for meeting the special learning needs of students. Three types of assistance are generally available:

Direct services

Indirect or consultative services

Related services

DIRECT SERVICES

Direct services are provided by working directly with students to correct or compensate for the conditions that have caused them to fall behind. Or in the case of students with exceptional gifts and talents, they are services that enrich or accelerate the students' progress through direct means. Teaching a student who is deaf to use sign language, a student with learning disabilities to read using a special method, or a fourth grader who is gifted to do algebra are examples of direct services provided by teachers.

INDIRECT SERVICES

Indirect services (or **consultative services**) are provided by special services personnel (e.g., special education teachers, school psychologists, and school social workers) and usually occur over a period of time. Special services personnel work with classroom teachers and others who work with exceptional students. Helping a general education teacher identify the best method for teaching a student with a learning disability to read or showing a teacher how to reposition a student who has a physical challenge are examples of indirect services provided by special services professionals.

RELATED SERVICES

Related services are both direct (to students) and indirect (services to those who then work with students). Related services are provided by specially trained personnel and include psychological testing and counseling, school social work, educational and occupational therapy, adapted physical education, school health services, and transportation.

7

Where Are Students Taught?

Some students in special education spend all their time in special education classrooms. Some, because of illness or other medical problems, are educated in hospitals or at home. And some students are taught in residential (institutional) settings in classes run and staffed by personnel from local school districts. Even when students require full-time special services, there are degrees of *restrictiveness.* In the most restrictive setting, students live in a residential school or institution and are taught by its staff members.

LEAST RESTRICTIVE ENVIRONMENT

The Individuals With Disabilities Education Improvement Act (IDEA, 2004) mandates a "free, appropriate public education" for all students with disabilities. Central to this provision is the concept of **least restrictive environment (LRE)**—that special education students should be educated in environments that are as much like general education, or are the least restrictive, as possible.

This does not mean that all students with disabilities must be placed in general education classrooms. It does mean, however, that students should spend as much time as possible in general education classes, ideally with their special needs met by indirect services. Some students may spend most of their time in the general classroom, leaving only for direct or related services. Others may spend the bulk of their time in special education classes, attending general classes for certain types of instructional activities, perhaps music or art.

The guiding principle in providing special education services is to move those with disabilities into less restrictive settings as much as possible in order to maximize opportunities for time and interactions with their natural neighbors and peers.

Participation in the general classroom is a form of equal opportunity. It gives students with disabilities a chance to share in experiences that those without disabilities get to have as a matter of course. These experiences are what really make education special.

How Does Diversity Influence Special Education?

Special education may seem to be a neat, orderly approach to helping students with special needs. It uses categories to organize students and curriculum. It sets criteria for eligibility. It defines each student's educational goals in a rational way. But it is unfair to teach you about special education without also teaching you about a few issues that are part and parcel of it.

Many of the concepts that are central to special education (e.g., categories, related services) are defined differently in different places. Moreover, no matter how convenient categories are, they mask both the similarities among students in different groups and the individual differences among students in the same groups. Then there are all the teaching methods and environments to think about. Understanding this diversity—the many different students and the many different environments in which special education is practiced—is central to understanding special education.

DIVERSE STUDENTS

Not all students who need special education services receive them, and those who do receive them are of various racial groups, categorical groups, geographical regions, and socioeconomic levels. The proportions of these groups in the population of students with special needs do not necessarily reflect their proportions in the general population; for example,

> Fifty one percent of students aged 3–21 who are enrolled in school are male, yet twice as many males as females are enrolled in special education programs.
>
> Seventy-five percent of the national school enrollment is white, but white students make up only 71 percent of the special education enrollment. In comparison, students who are black make up 16 percent of public school enrollment but 21 percent of the enrollment in special education programs. (National Research Council, 2002; President's Commission on Excellence in Special Education, 2002; U.S. Department of Education, 2001, 2002)

Variation is also evident in the numbers of students in different categories who receive special education services and in the numbers of specific categories served in states. For example, more students with learning disabilities are served than almost all other groups of exceptional students combined (U.S. Department of Education, 2002). About 90 percent of exceptional students are categorized with specific learning disabilities, speech or language impairments, mental retardation, or emotional disturbance. Less than 1 percent of them are categorized as deaf or blind or physically impaired. Twice as many students with learning disabilities are educated in some states as are educated in neighboring states.

Dropping Out

Many students do not receive special education because they are not in school. In the United States, about 10 percent of all students drop out of school each year. Drop-out rates for white students are below 5 percent while rates for some ethnic groups are much higher. For example, 15 percent of the black population, 20 percent of Hispanics, and 22 percent of Native

Americans leave school without finishing (National Center for Education Statistics, 1997).

Drop-Out Rates of Students With Special Needs

About 30 percent of students with disabilities drop out of school (U.S. Department of Education, 2002). Since 1995–1996, most disability categories experienced an improvement in drop-out rate. One notable exception was students in the deaf-blindness category who experienced an increase in drop-out rate between 1995–1996 and 1999–2000. Of course, deaf-blindness is one of the smallest disability categories, and its drop-out rate varies widely from one year to the next; in 1995–1996 and 1997–1998, the drop-out rate for students with deaf-blindness was notably lower than in other years (U.S. Department of Education, 2002). The most improvement in the drop-out rate in recent years was evident in the speech or language impairments, specific learning disabilities, orthopedic impairments, hearing impairments, and emotional disturbance categories (U.S. Department of Education, 2002).

DIVERSE EDUCATIONAL SETTINGS

According to Public Law 94–142 (now IDEA), exceptional students must be educated in the least restrictive environment. In recent years, this has meant that most exceptional students have received special education and related services in schools with their peers without disabilities. Here, too, we find variation in the extent to which students in the various categories are placed in specific settings. For example, although about 65 percent of students with language impairments are served in general education classrooms, fewer than 10 percent of students with mental retardation, emotional disturbance, deafness, or blindness are served there. Most students with mental retardation (55 percent) are served in separate classes, as are at least

35 percent of those with emotional disturbance and multiple disabilities. But less than 25 percent of students with specific learning disabilities, visual impairments, deafness, and blindness are placed in special classes (U.S. Department of Education, 2001, 2002).

VARIATIONS BY STATE

Learning environments also vary by state. Fewer than 10 percent of children aged 3–21 are served in general education classes in nine states, but more than 30 percent are served in general education classes in 25 states. Less than 10 percent of students with learning disabilities are served in separate classes in 17 states, but less than 10 percent of students with speech impairments are placed in these settings in 37 states (U.S. Department of Education, 2000, 2001, 2002). Overall, very few students who are deaf, blind, or physically impaired are served in separate facilities, but some states use this option much more than others. More than twice as many students with learning disabilities are educated in general education classes in some states than in neighboring states.

What About Students Who Are Gifted and Talented?

W hile a large number of students in any school may be seen as smart, only a few are formally identified as gifted and talented. The term *gifted and talented* is used to designate people who are intellectually, creatively, academically, or otherwise superior to a comparison group of peers or older people. The term *gifted* usually refers to students with superior intellectual or cognitive performance, while the term *talented* usually refers to students who show outstanding performance in a specific area, such as the performing or visual arts.

Unlike the other special education categories, gifted and talented is not included in Public Law 94–142 or the Individuals With Disabilities Education Act. Separate legislation, the Gifted and Talented Children's Education Act of 1978, gives states financial incentives to develop programs for students considered gifted and talented. The legislation includes the following definition of gifted and talented children:

> The term "gifted and talented" means children, and whenever applicable, youth who are identified at the preschool, elementary, or secondary level as possessing demonstrated or potential abilities, that give evidence of high performance capability in areas such as intellectual,

creative, specific academic, or leadership ability, or in the performing and visual arts and who by reason thereof require services or activities not ordinarily provided by the school.

A brief description of each area of giftedness or talent follows to help you understand the students identified by this definition.

INTELLECTUAL ABILITY

Laypersons and educators alike usually define **intellectual ability** in terms of a high score on an intelligence test—usually two standard deviations above the mean—on individual or group measures. Parents and teachers often recognize students with general intellectual talent by their wide-ranging fund of general information and high levels of vocabulary, memory, abstract word knowledge, and abstract reasoning.

CREATIVE ABILITY

Students with high **creative ability** produce new ideas by bringing together elements usually thought of as independent or dissimilar and by developing new meanings that have social value. Characteristics of creative students include openness to experience, setting personal standards for evaluation, ability to play with ideas, willingness to take risks, preference for complexity, tolerance for ambiguity, positive self-image, and the ability to become immersed in a task.

SPECIFIC ACADEMIC ABILITY

Students with **specific academic ability** are identified by their outstanding performance on an achievement or aptitude test in one area, such as mathematics or language arts. The organizers of talent searches sponsored by a number of universities and colleges identify students with specific academic aptitude who score at the 97th percentile or higher on standard achievement tests.

LEADERSHIP ABILITY

Those with high **leadership ability** direct individuals or groups to a common decision or action. Students who demonstrate giftedness in leadership ability use group skills and negotiate in difficult situations. Many teachers recognize leadership through a student's keen interest and skill in problem solving. Leadership characteristics include self-confidence, responsibility, cooperation, a tendency to dominate, and the ability to adapt readily to new situations.

ABILITY IN THE VISUAL
AND PERFORMING ARTS

Students with high **ability in the visual and performing arts** demonstrate special talents in visual art, music, dance, drama, or other related studies. Talented students need to learn that their abilities can create for them a unique and enduring place in the world. The talented, young painter Alexandra Nechita put it well:

> Sometimes I get so immersed in my paintings I'm just somewhere else. I create my own universe that you get to see little by little through every painting I work at. And every painting I create is part of me going out little by little to all of you. (Nechita, 1996, p. 80)

IDENTIFYING GIFTS AND TALENTS

Callahan, Hunsaker, Adams, Moore, and Bland (1995) compiled a review of identification practices and offered the following guidelines for identifying students who are gifted and talented:

1. Adopt a clear but broad definition of giftedness.

2. Use standardized tests and checklists, process and performance indicators, and multiple sources of data (e.g., student, teacher, parent, peers) to get the most complete picture of the student being identified.

3. Use separate measures for different areas of giftedness (e.g., intellectual vs. creative ability).

4. Assess all abilities using instruments that are reliable and valid.

5. Screen and identify students without using single cutoff scores or summed matrix scores.

6. Use nontraditional methods for effective identification of underserved populations who may manifest giftedness in different ways.

7. Identify based on needs of individual students, not on quotas.

The challenge of educating students who are gifted and talented is twofold. First, students with demonstrated or potential abilities must be identified early in their academic careers. Second, students who are gifted and talented must have a full-service education if we expect them to thrive and succeed in and out of school. This means that students who are gifted and talented must be involved in educational experiences that are challenging and appropriate to their needs and performance levels. For many students, these challenges are met in special education programs.

10

Special Education in Perspective

S pecial education is many things to many people. To parents, special education promises help, a means for their children to reach their full potential. As members of the special education team, parents are part of the decision-making process. They have a say in how their children are served.

Students react to their special education in specific ways at various stages of the process. Initially, they may think that *special* means *different* in a bad way, that the services are a kind of punishment for their inability to do certain things. But if their individualized programs help them master academic, social, and personal skills, their negative feelings about special education usually fall away.

For general education teachers and administrators, special education is simply a method for assisting students who need help to be successful in school. To some special educators, special education is a separate system for educating exceptional students, but to most, it is a process that is an integral part of the general education system.

All students—both exceptional and non-exceptional—are more alike than they are different. They need to interact, to share experiences. The importance of that interaction for exceptional students is clear: To learn to act in expected ways, they must be exposed to expected behaviors. But this interaction is equally important for those who are not exceptional. With it comes an understanding of how little the differences matter, of how much alike all people are. And with that understanding comes acceptance.

11

What Have We Learned?

A s you complete your study of the fundamentals of special education, it may be helpful to review what you have learned. To help you check your understanding of the fundamentals, we have listed the key points and key vocabulary for you to review. We have included the Self-Assessment again so you can compare what you know now with what you knew as you began your study. Finally, we provide a few topics for you to think about and some activities for you to do on your own.

KEY POINTS

◙ Special education addresses the special learning needs of students, helping them reach their full potentials in school.

◙ IDEA protects the rights of students with disabilities, guaranteeing them an "appropriate public education."

◙ The categories of special education represent different kinds of learning needs.

◙ The number of students receiving special education has increased steadily in recent years; today, more than 6 million students are enrolled in special education programs.

◙ Students with special needs must be declared eligible for services before those services can be provided in public school programs.

◙ The types of services students receive as part of a special education program vary according to the level of their special needs.

◙ The law mandates that students with special needs be taught in the least restrictive environment.

◙ Despite structured categories and educational plans, special education is a diverse field.

◙ The belief that all students are more alike than they are different is shaping contemporary practices in special education today.

KEY VOCABULARY

Ability in the visual and performing arts is inferred from an individual's special talents in visual art, music, dance, drama, or other related studies.

Autism is a category used to describe individuals who have special learning needs in areas related to verbal and nonverbal communication and social interaction.

Blindness or Visual Impairment is a category used to describe individuals who have special learning needs in areas requiring functional use of vision.

Consultative services (or indirect services) are provided by special services personnel (e.g., special education teachers, school psychologists, and school social workers) and usually occur over a period of time.

Creative ability is inferred from an individual's efforts to produce new ideas by bringing together elements usually thought of as independent or dissimilar and by developing new meanings that have social value.

Deafness and Blindness is a category used to describe individuals who have special learning needs in areas requiring functional use of hearing *and* vision.

Deafness or Hearing Impairment is a category used to describe individuals who have special learning needs in areas requiring functional use of hearing. Less than 1 percent of the school-aged population is classified in this category.

Direct services are provided by working directly with students to correct or compensate for the conditions that have caused them to fall behind.

Due Process provisions protect the rights of students with disabilities under the same legal provisions that protect the rights of students without disabilities.

Education is the process of learning and changing as a result of schooling and other experiences.

Emotional Disturbance is a category used to describe individuals who have special learning needs in areas requiring functional use of social and emotional skills.

Exceptional students are those who have disabilities or extraordinary gifts and talents.

Gifted and Talented is a category used to describe individuals who have special learning needs in areas requiring functional use of intelligence and artistic ability.

Inclusion is the practice of educating students with exceptionalities in general education classrooms.

Indirect services (or consultative services) are provided by special services personnel (e.g., special education teachers, school psychologists, and school social workers) and usually occur over a period of time.

Individualized Education Programs (IEPs) are well-planned school programs tailored to meet students' unique learning needs.

Intellectual ability is inferred from an individual's score on an intelligence test.

Leadership ability is inferred from an individual's efforts to direct individuals or groups to a common decision or action.

Least Restrictive Environment provisions protect the right of students with disabilities to be educated as much as possible in environments like those provided students without disabilities.

Mental Retardation is a category used to describe individuals who have special learning needs in areas requiring functional use of intelligence and adaptive behavior.

Multiple or Severe Disabilities is a category used to describe individuals who have special learning needs in more than one area requiring functional use of skills.

Orthopedic or Other Health Impairments is a category used to describe individuals who have special learning needs in areas requiring functional use of hands, arms, legs, feet, and other body parts.

Prereferral intervention is the process of finding ways to keep exceptional students in general education classrooms before referring them for special education services.

Protection in Evaluation Procedures protects the right of students with disabilities to have decisions made about them in an unbiased manner.

Referral is the process of requesting information to decide if a student is eligible for special education services.

Related services are provided by specially trained personnel and include psychological testing and counseling, school social work, educational or occupational therapy, adapted physical education, school health services, and transportation.

Special education is instruction designed for students with special learning needs.

Specific academic ability is inferred from an individual's performance on an achievement or aptitude test in one area, such as mathematics or language arts.

Specific Learning Disabilities is a category used to describe individuals who have special learning needs in areas requiring functional use of listening, speaking, reading, writing, reasoning, and arithmetic skills.

Speech or Language Impairments is a category used to describe individuals who have special learning needs in areas requiring functional use of language and communication skills.

Traumatic Brain Injury is a category used to describe individuals who have special learning needs in areas related to injuries to the brain that result in total or partial loss of ability or psychosocial adjustment. The injuries adversely affect their educational performance. This category does not include brain injuries that are congenital or degenerative or those induced by birth trauma. Less than 1 percent of the school-aged population is classified in this category.

Self-Assessment 2

After you finish this book, check your knowledge of the content covered. Choose the best answer for each of the following questions.

1. The educational system that is an alternative to the general education system is

   a. Special education

   b. Gifted and talented education

   c. Compulsory education

   d. Separated education

2. The year 2000 marked the _____ anniversary of federal legislation mandating a free, appropriate public education for individuals with disabilities.

   a. 10th

   b. 25th

   c. 50th

   d. 100th

3. Federal law does not require states to provide special education to

   a. Students with emotional problems

   b. Students who are over the age of 21

   c. Students who are in preschool

   d. Students who are in high school

4. Special education services are provided to approximately
   _____ students each year.

   a. 2 million

   b. 4 million

   c. 6 million

   d. 8 million

5. Federal laws were passed to protect the rights of individuals with disabilities because

   a. They were not being treated the same as their peers without disabilities.

   b. They were performing below expectations when compared to their peers without disabilities.

   c. They were entitled to special services by laws written in the 1800s but forgotten in recent times.

   d. They were entitled to special services by state laws governing education.

6. To receive special education, a child must be declared eligible for services in at least one of _____ categories accepted by the federal government and most states.

   a. 3

   b. 5

   c. 11

   d. 13

7. The process of requesting information to decide if a student is eligible for special education services is called
   _____.

   a. Referral

   b. Examination

c. Opportunity to learn

d. Intervention

8. Direct, indirect, and related are all

   a. Types of general education interventions

   b. Types of special education services

   c. Types of counseling for students who are gifted and talented

   d. Prereferral interventions

9. The guiding principle of special education that directs that students should be educated in environments as much like general education as possible is known as

   a. Inclusive education

   b. Opportunity to learn

   c. Least restrictive environment

   d. Educational due process

10. The prevailing belief about special education today is that

   a. All students are more alike than they are different.

   b. All students need special education at some time in their lives.

   c. Special education should be provided in self-contained classrooms for most children requiring special education services.

   d. Special education services should be available to more children than are currently being served.

REFLECTION

After you answer the multiple-choice questions, think about how you would answer the following questions:

- What is special education and whom does it serve?
- What does IDEA mandate?
- What is inclusion and what does it mean for teachers?

Answer Key for Self-Assessments

1. a

2. b

3. b

4. c

5. a

6. c

7. a

8. b

9. c

10. a

On Your Own

☑ Interview three teachers. Ask them to define special education and to provide two examples of students they believe should be provided special services.

☑ Make a list of the kinds of categories in which students in your state are eligible to receive special education services. Identify how your state's department of education defines each category.

☑ Start a scrapbook of newspaper and magazine articles about people with exceptionalities and their educational experiences.

☑ Find an introductory special education textbook and list the definitions it provides for *special education* and *exceptional students.*

☑ Interview two teachers and ask how they define *disability.* Have the teachers describe the behaviors they use to tell the differences between different disabilities.

Resources

BOOKS

Rawson, M. J. (2000). *A manual of special education law for educators and parents.* Naples, FL: Morgen. This book is appropriate for school district personnel, those preparing for careers in special education, and parents of students receiving special education. It provides an overview of special education law, including IDEA and its subsequent amendments.

Yell, M. (1998). *The law and special education.* Upper Saddle River, NJ: Prentice Hall. This book helps readers understand the procedures and practices of legal research, using a variety of sources. Readers are acquainted with legal development of special education and the current legal requirements of providing a free, appropriate public education for students with disabilities. It is an excellent resource on the law and special education.

Ysseldyke, J. E., Algozzine, B., & Thurlow, M. L. (2000). *Critical issues in special and remedial education.* Boston: Houghton Mifflin. The state of the art in any field should be evaluated periodically. This book is a comprehensive analysis of critical issues in the provision of special services for individuals with disabilities. It is a straightforward review of conceptual and practical concerns that face professionals involved in all aspects of special education. The text does not offer solutions to all problems that are identified, but it does a good job of documenting critical areas and the kinds of questions that need to be asked when evaluating special education.

Journals and Articles

Algozzine, B., & Ysseldyke, J. (1987). Questioning discrepancies: Retaking the first step twenty years later. *Learning Disability Quarterly, 10,* 301–313. The authors challenge the practice of defining learning disabilities on the basis of discrepancies between ability and achievement. They demonstrate that it is relatively common to find large discrepancies among students who are not formally identified with learning disabilities. The article illustrates that definitional issues in special education have been addressed in the wrong way.

Davis, W. E. (1989). The regular education initiative debate: Its promises and problems. *Exceptional Children, 55,* 440–446. The most intense issue receiving attention in the special education professional literature at the time this article was published was the regular education initiative (REI) debate (i.e., providing instruction for students with disabilities in classrooms with their natural neighbors and peers). Davis examines the arguments, identifies specific problems and issues, and suggests strategies for overcoming perceived obstacles and improving dialogue.

Greer, J. V. (1988). Cultural diversity and the test of leadership. *Exceptional Children, 55,* 199–201. Greer describes the cultural diversity of United States schools in the 1980s and the promise of the growing concern for leadership in the profession of special education. Today, cultural diversity is one of special education's major issues. Students from diverse backgrounds are disproportionately represented in special education, a fact that has led many to examine assessment processes that are for the most part woefully inadequate. Furthermore, continuing shortages of personnel qualified to assess and teach these students have created crisis conditions in many states.

Hallahan, D. P., & Kauffman, J. M. (1977). Labels, categories, behaviors: ED, LD, and EMR reconsidered. *Journal of Special Education, 11,* 139–149. The authors argue that there are few functional differences in the behaviors of students with emotional disturbance, learning disabilities, and educable mental retardation. They offer valid criticisms of labeling and categorizing students. This article is frequently cited by professionals interested in non-categorical or cross-categorical approaches to providing special education.

Lipsky, D. K., & Gartner, A. (1989). *Beyond separate education: Quality education for all*. Baltimore: Brookes. This compilation of original articles argues that all exceptional students are entitled to effective educational programs. Included are chapters on the passage of Public Law 94–142, a history of effective school research, and the thoughts of students who have received special services. The book has been widely used by those interested in inclusion.

Reynolds, M. C., & Balow, B. (1972). Categories and variables in special education. *Exceptional Children, 38*, 357–366. The authors describe the negative nature of the categories and labels (impaired, disordered, disturbed) used to identify exceptional students. This is one of the earliest articles to call into question the practice of placing people into categories and labeling their disabilities.

ORGANIZATIONS

National Information Center for Children and Youth with Disabilities (NICHCY) is the national information center that provides information on disabilities and disability-related issues. They have many publications in English and Spanish. NICHCY, P.O. Box 1492; Washington, DC 20013; (800) 695–0285 (Voice/TTY); nichcy@aed.org; *www.nichcy.org*; http://www.nichcy.org

References

Callahan, C. M., Hunsaker, S. L., Adams, C. M., Moore, S. D., & Bland, L. C. (1995). *Instruments used in the identification of gifted and talented students* (Research Monograph 95130). Storrs, CT: The National Research Center on the Gifted and Talented, University of Connecticut.

Education for All Handicapped Children Act, Pub. L. N. 94–142, 89 stat. 773 (1975).

ERIC Clearinghouse on Disabilities and Gifted Education. (2001). *Educating exceptional children: A statistical profile.* Arlington, VA: Council of Exceptional Children.

Gifted and Talented Children's Education Act, U.S. Pub. L. N. 95–561 §902 (1978).

Individuals With Disabilities Education Improvement Act, L. N. 108–446 (2004). Retrieved December 20, 2005, from www.ed.gov

National Center for Education Statistics. (1997). *Dropout rates in the United States: 1996.* Washington, DC: Author.

National Research Council. (2002). *Minority students in special and gifted education* (M. S. Donovan & C. T. Cross, Eds.). Washington, DC: National Academy Press.

Nechita, A. (1996). *Outside the lines: Paintings by Alexandra Nechita.* Atlanta, GA: Longstreet.

President's Commission on Excellence in Special Education. (2002). *A new era: Revitalizing special education for children and their families.* Washington, DC: Author.

U.S. Department of Education. (2000). *Twenty-second annual report to Congress on the Implementation of the Individuals With Disabilities Education Act.* Washington, DC: Author.

U.S. Department of Education. (2001). *Twenty-third annual report to Congress on the implementation of the Individuals With Disabilities Education Act.* Washington, DC: Author.

U.S. Department of Education. (2002). *Twenty-fourth annual report to Congress on the implementation of the Individuals With Disabilities Education Act.* Washington, DC: Author.

Index

Note: Numbers in **Bold** followed by a colon [:] denote the book number within which the page numbers are found.

AAMR (American Association on Mental Retardation), **12:**6, **12:**20–21, **12:**66

Ability training, 4:39–40, 4:62

Academic achievement, assessing, **3:**37–39
achievement tests, **3:**37, **3:**77
interviews, **3:**38–39
observations, **3:**38
portfolios, **3:**39

Academic engaged time, **3:**22–23, **3:**76

Academic learning disabilities, **9:**51

Academic time analysis, **3:**22–23, **3:**76

Acceleration or advancement, **13:**25–27, **13:**36–40, **13:**52

Acceptability, **3:**56–57

Accommodations
defining, **3:**77
for student with sensory disabilities, 7:49–51
in general education classrooms, 1:21–22
without patronization, 4:14

See also Instruction, adapting for students with special needs

Accountability, **3:**17, **3:**77
outcomes-based, **3:**23, **6:**35

Acculturation, **3:**63, **3:**77

Achievement tests, **3:**37, **3:**77

Acting out, **3:**47

Active observation, **3:**29, **3:**77

Adams, C. M., **1:**35–36

Adaptive behavior, **3:**41–43, **3:**77
defining, **12:**21
environmental effects on, **3:**42–43
mental retardation and, **12:**17, **12:**19–25, **12:**21 (tab)–23 (tab), **12:**45–49

Adaptive behavior scales, **3:**42, **12:**71

Adaptive devices, **8:**52, **8:**62–63

ADHD. *See* Attention deficit hyperactivity disorder

Adult literacy/lifelong learning, **5:**50, **6:**27–28

Advanced Placement (AP), **13:**26

Advocacy groups, **6:**11, **6:**12–13, **6:**44

Ahlgren, C., **12:**67
AIDS, **5:**10, **8:**12–13, **8:**58–59, **8:**63
Aim line, **4:**29, **4:**63
Alcohol-/drug-free schools,
    6:28–29
Algozzine, B., **4:**5, **6:**9, **12:**62
Alley, G., **4:**45
Allocation of funds, **6:**15,
    6:16–17, **6:**44
Allsop, J., **8:**49
Alternative living unit (ALU),
    5:31, **5:**54
Alternative-print format, **3:**71
Alternatives for recording
    answers, **3:**71
Amendments to the Education
    for All Handicapped
    Children Act, **2:**11 (tab)
Amendments to the Individuals
    With Disabilities Education
    Act, **2:**12 (tab), **2:**27–29
American Association on Mental
    Retardation (AAMR),
    12:6, **12:**11, **12:**18–19,
    12:20–21, **12:**66
American Asylum for the
    Education and Instruction
    of the Deaf, **2:**9–10
American Federation of
    Teachers, **6:**11
American Psychiatric
    Association, **9:**44
American Sign Language (ASL),
    7:40, **7:**59
American Speech-Language-
    Hearing Association
    (ASHA), **10:**10, **10:**35
Americans With Disabilities Act
    (ADA), **2:**12 (tab), **2:**26–27,
    2:54, **8:**49
Amplification systems, **4:**51, **7:**41
Analysis error, **3:**38, **3:**78
Analytical programs, **9:**27, **9:**56
Antia, S. D., **7:**26

Anxiety, **11:**18–22, **11:**46
AP (Advanced Placement), **13:**26
Apprenticeships programs,
    5:45, **5:**56
Appropriate education,
    2:42 (tab), **2:**46, **2:**54
ARC (Association for Retarded
    Citizens), **12:**66
Architectural accessibility,
    2:14, **2:**54
Articulation disorder,
    10:9–10, **10:**43
Asch, A., **7:**33–34
ASHA (American
    Speech-Language-Hearing
    Association), **10:**10, **10:**35
Assessment
    academic achievement,
        3:37–39
    alternatives for recording
        answers, **3:**71
    classroom, **3:**73–74
    curriculum-based, **3:**19–21,
        3:78, **9:**19
    data collection for, **3:**25–31
    defining, **3:**77
    ecobehavioral, **3:**22–23, **3:**78
    effects of, **3:**74
    error and, **3:**62–63
    formal, **3:**11
    functional academic,
        9:19, **9:**57
    functional behavioral, **9:**19,
        9:57, **11:**15–16, **11:**47
    instructional environments,
        3:23, **3:**77
    needs, **4:**41, **4:**64
    portfolios, **3:**26, **3:**39, **3:**80
    prereferral interventions, **3:**11
    psychoeducational, **3:**9, **3:**81
    psychological development,
        3:45–47
    skilled examiner for,
        3:59–61

work-sample, **3:**26, **3:**81
See also Assessment
    guidelines; Assessment
    practices; Data collection;
    Protection in evaluation
    procedures
Assessment,
    decision-making and
    accountability, **3:**17
    child-study team role in,
        3:12–15
    eligibility/entitlement,
        3:14–15
    exceptionality decisions, **3:**12
    instructional planning, **3:**15
    intervention assistance, **3:**10
    overview of, **3:**8 (tab)
    program evaluation, **3:**16–17
    progress evaluation, **3:**15–16
    psychoeducational
        assessment referral, **3:**9
    screening decisions, **3:**7–10
    special help/enrichment, **3:**10
    special learning needs,
        3:13–14
Assessment guidelines, **3:**65–71
    accommodation, **3:**71
    environment, **3:**70–71
    frequency, **3:**69
    improving instruction, **3:**69
    more than describing
        problems, **3:**67–69
    no one cause of school
        problems, **3:**66
    no right way to assess, **3:**66
    variables, **3:**70
Assessment practices, **3:**17–24
    curriculum-based assessment,
        3:19–21
    curriculum-based
        measurement, **3:**21–22
    instructional diagnosis, **3:**22
    instructional
        environments, **3:**23

outcomes-based
    accountability, **3:**23
performance assessment, **3:**24
See also Reliability;
    Representativeness;
    Validity
Assisted listening devices,
    7:39 (tab), **7:**41, **7:**42
Assistive technologies,
    2:26, **7:**13, **7:**52
Association for Retarded
    Citizens (ARC), **12:**66
Asthma, **8:**9–10, **8:**11 (tab), **8:**63
Astigmatism, **7:**10, **7:**59
At risk student, **2:**24, **3:**8, **3:**9,
    5:14–15, **6:**20, **13:**14
Ataxic cerebral palsy, **8:**24
Athetoid cerebral palsy, **8:**24
Attack strategy training,
    4:40, **4:**63
Attention deficit
    hyperactivity disorder
    (ADHD), **2:**15, **8:**34
    criteria for, **9:**44 (tab)–45 (tab)
    defining, **9:**43–46, **9:**56
    remediating, **9:**46–48
Audio aids, **7:**36 (tab)
Audiometer, **3:**40, **3:**77
Auditory acuity, **7:**19, **7:**59
Autism, **1:**15–16, **1:**40, **8:**17,
    8:28–31, **8:**63
Automaticity, **4:**20, **4:**63
Auxiliary aids, **2:**14

Bain, J. D., **4:**5
Barnett, S., **5:**16
Barraga, N. C., **7:**8
Basic skills, **9:**56
Batshaw, M. L., **8:**22, **8:**47
Beattie v. State Board of Education,
    2:36 (tab)
Behavior intervention plan,
    11:16, **11:**46
Behavior therapy, **4:**38, **4:**63

Bennett, T., **3:**21
Berdine, W. H., **8:**46
Berrueta-Clement, J., **5:**16
Biklen, D., **6:**41
Bingo (game), **12:**40 (fig)
Blackhurst, A. E., **8:**46
Blackorby, J., **5:**24
Bland, L. C., **1:**35–36
Blindisms, **7:**14
Blindness, **1:**16
   defining, **1:**40, **7:**8–9, **7:**59
   See also Braille; Visual
      impairments
Bloom, B., **4:**41
Books (resources)
   assessment, **3:**91–92
   communication
      disorders, **10:**57
   effective instruction, **4:**75–76
   emotional disturbance,
      11:57–60
   fundamentals of special
      education, **1:**53
   gifted and talented child,
      13:63–64
   learning disabilities, **9:**67
   legal foundations, **2:**65–66
   medical/physical/multiple
      disabilities, **8:**75–80
   mental retardation, **12:**81–84
   public policy/school
      reform, **6:**55
   sensory disabilities, **7:**73–77
   transitions, **5:**65–67
Bounty hunting, **6:**17
Braille, **4:**52, **7:**10, **7:**13, **7:**15, **7:**16,
   7:34, **7:**35 (tab)
Braille display technology,
   7:37, **7:**59
Braille note-taking devices, **7:**38
Braille printers, **7:**37, **7:**59
Brailler, **4:**52, **4:**63
Brooks-Gunn, J., **5:**15
Brophy, J., **4:**13

Brown, F., **3:**62–63
Brown, L., **12:**55, **12:**67
Brown v. Board of Education,
   2:35, **2:**36 (tab), **2:**44
Bryant, B., **3:**37
Bureau of Indian Affairs,
   6:11, **6:**13
Burlington School Committee
   v. Massachusetts Board of
   Education, **2:**42 (tab), **2:**46–47
Byrnes, L. J., **7:**26

Callahan, C. M., **1:**35–36
Cameto, R., **5:**24
Cancer, **8:**11 (tab), **8:**63
Canes, for students with visual
   impairments, **4:**55
Carrow-Woolfolk, E., **10:**26
Carta, J., **3:**22, **4:**46
Carter, K., **7:**38
Cartwright, C., **4:**53
Cartwright, G., **4:**53
Case, L. P., **9:**17–18
Categorical programs,
   1:17, **6:**16, **6:**44
CCTV (closed-circuit television),
   7:35 (tab), **7:**36–37
CEC (Council for Exceptional
   Children), **12:**66
Cefalu v. East Baton Rouge
   Parish School Board,
   2:43 (tab)–44 (tab)
Center-based programs,
   5:13, **5:**14, **5:**54
Cerebral palsy, **8:**23–24, **8:**63
CHADD, **9:**46
Chadsey-Rusch, J., **5:**24
Chalfant, J. C., **9:**51
Chang, S. C., **7:**15
Child-find programs,
   7:30, **7:**59
Child-study team, **3:**12–15, **3:**77
Choate, J., **3:**21
Christenson, S. L., **3:**14, **3:**23

Citizens Concerned About Disability, **6:**11

Civil Rights Act, **2:**26

Clark, B., **4:**41

Classification
changes in practices, **6:**8–9
defining, **6:**44

Classroom amplification systems, **7:**41, **7:**51

Classroom assessment, **3:**73–74

Classwide peer tutoring, **4:**47, **4:**63

Client-centered therapy, **4:**43–44, **4:**63

Cloninger, C., **12:**59

Close-captioned television, **4:**51

Closed-circuit television (CCTV), **7:**35 (tab), **7:**36–37

Coefficient, reliability, **3:**50, **3:**81

Cognitive behavior modification, **4:**41, **4:**63

Cognitive mapping, **7:**34

Cognitive skills training, **4:**41, **4:**43

Cohen, H. J., **8:**13

Coleman, M. C., **11:**36

Coleman, M. R., **13:**11, **13:**45

Committee for Economic Development, **5:**14–15

Communication boards, **4:**50, **8:**41, **8:**63

Communication disorders
academic characteristics of, **10:**14
behavioral characteristics of, **10:**15
cognitive characteristics of, **10:**13–14
combating negative stereotypes about, **10:**37 (tab)–38
communication characteristics of, **10:**15–16
defining, **10:**43

fluency problems, **10:**16
identifying, **10:**24–27
language disorders, **10:**10–11
language problems, **10:**16
phonology/morphology/ syntax problems, **10:**10–11
physical characteristics of, **10:**14–15
pragmatics problems, **10:**11
pulling students from classroom, **10:**36–37
semantics problems, **10:**11
speech disorders, **10:**9–10
team approach to providing services, **10:**35–36
tips to improve communication, **10:**38
voice problems, **10:**15
See also Communication disorders, teaching students with

Communication disorders, teaching students with, **10:**17–30
interpersonal problems, **10:**27–30
language problems, **10:**20–27
speech problems, **10:**18–20
tips for teachers, **10:**19 (tab)
trends/issues influencing, **10:**31–33

Communication skills, **3:**42

Communication/motility. *See* Instructional adaptations, to increase

Community collaboration, **5:**7, **5:**43–46, **5:**55, **13:**48

Compensatory education, **3:**10, **3:**77

Competitive employment, **5:**24–25, **5:**55

Computer-assisted instruction, **4:**5

Concentration game, **12:**41 (fig)

Concussion, **8**:25–26, **8**:63
Conductive hearing loss,
　　7:19, **7**:59
Conlon, C. J., **8**:14
Consultative (indirect) services,
　　1:26, **1**:40, **1**:41, **5**:12, **5**:55
Contextual variables, **4**:10, **4**:63
Continued education, **5**:26–27
Contusions, **8**:26, **8**:63
Convergent thinking,
　　13:17–18, **13**:52
Cooperative learning,
　　4:45–46, **4**:63
Corn, A., **7**:15
Corrective/supportive feedback,
　　4:40, **4**:46–47, **12**:37, **12**:43
Council for Children With
　　Behavioral Disorders, **11**:36
Council for Exceptional Children
　　(CEC), **12**:66
Counseling therapy,
　　4:43–45, **4**:63
*Covarrubias v. San Diego Unified
　　School District*, **2**:38 (tab)
Craniofacial anomalies,
　　8:22, **8**:63
Creative ability, **1**:34, **1**:40–41
Creative-productive giftedness,
　　13:43, **13**:52
Creech, B., **7**:26, **7**:42
Crisis therapy, **4**:44–45, **4**:63
Criterion-referenced tests,
　　3:28–29, **3**:77–78, **4**:9, **4**:64
Critical thinking, **4**:43
Crittenden, J. B.,
　　7:87
Crocker, A. C., **8**:13
Cued speech, **7**:39 (tab),
　　7:40–41, **7**:42
Cues
　　auditory, **7**:16, **7**:28, **7**:43
　　defining, **9**:56
　　phonetic, **9**:29, **9**:57
　　to improve math, **9**:32

　　to improve work
　　　habits, **9**:36
　　to reduce behavior problems,
　　　10:37, **11**:24
Curriculum compacting,
　　13:39, **13**:40
Curriculum-based assessment,
　　3:19–21, **3**:78, **9**:19
Curriculum-based measurement,
　　3:21–22, **3**:78
Curriculum-referenced tests. *See*
　　Criterion-referenced tests
Currie, J., **5**:15
Cystic fibrosis, **8**:12, **8**:63

D'Allura, T., **7**:14
D'Amico, R., **5**:24
Data collection, for assessments,
　　3:25–31
Davidson, J. E., **13**:43
Davis, L., **12**:67
Deaf
　　defining, **7**:18, **7**:21, **7**:59
　　See also Deaf-and-blind/
　　　deaf-blind; Hearing
　　　impairments
Deaf culture, **7**:26, **7**:59
Deaf-and-blind/deaf-blind
　　characteristics of, **7**:31–32
　　defining, **7**:29–30, **7**:59–60
　　prevalence of, **7**:30
Deafness and blindness,
　　1:16, **1**:41, **7**:6, **7**:60
Deafness or hearing impairment,
　　1:16, **1**:41
Deinstitutionalization,
　　5:30, **5**:55
Delquadri, J., **4**:46
Dennis, R., **12**:59
Deno, S. L., **3**:22
Denton, P., **4**:45
Deshler, D., **4**:45
Developmental learning
　　disabilities, **9**:51

Diabetes, **8:**11 (tab), **8:**63

Diagnostic tests, **3:**28, **3:**78

Diana v. State Board of Education,
    2:37 (tab)

Direct instruction,
    principles of, **4:**64
    corrective/supportive
        feedback, **4:**40, **4:**46–47,
        12:37, **12:**43
    independent practice,
        4:40, **10:**36–37
    modeling expected
        behavior, **4:**40
    task analysis, **3:**22, **3:**81,
        4:10, **4:**40, **4:**65,
        12:43–45, **12:**72
    See also Instruction

Direct services, **1:**25, **1:**41,
    5:12, **5:**55

Discrepancy
    defining, **9:**56
    dual, **9:**17–18
    eliminating, **9:**9

Discrepant scores, **3:**34,
    3:78, **12:**30

Discrimination, protection
    against, **1:**13

Distractibility (nonattention),
    3:47, **11:**47

Disturbed peer relations, **3:**47

Divergent thinking, **13:**17, **13:**52

Diverse students, **1:**29–31

Doorlag, D. H., **10:**18–20

Down syndrome, **12:**13–14,
    12:66, **12:**71

Drop out rate, **1:**30–31

Drug addiction, pregnancy and,
    5:10, **8:**14–15

DSM-IV, **9:**45 (tab)

Dual discrepancy, **9:**17–18

Due process, **1:**13, **1:**41, **2:**21,
    2:54, **2:**55

Duhaime, A., **8:**25, **8:**26, **8:**27

Dunn, Leota M., **10:**27

Dunn, Lloyd M., **10:**27

Duration recording, **3:**46, **3:**78

Early intervention
    as part of lifelong
        learning, **5:**50
    defining, **2:**55, **5:**55, **6:**44
    direct/indirect services for,
        5:12
    effectiveness of, **5:**14–16
    federal laws/incentives
        for, **5:**11–12
    for infants/toddlers, **2:**24
    Head Start, **5:**15
    home-based programs,
        5:12–13
    hospital-/center-based
        programs, **5:**13–14
    need for more
        programs, **5:**10
    preschool, **5:**9–10
    social factor influence on,
        6:9–10
    special education services,
        5:10–11 (fig)
    Ypsilanti Perry Preschool
        Project, **5:**15–16

E-books, **9:**29

Echolalia, **8:**41, **11:**14

Ecobehavioral assessment,
    3:22–23, **3:**78

Edelman, S., **12:**59

Education, defining, **1:**9, **1:**41

Education for All Handicapped
    Children Act, **1:**12;
    2:11 (tab), **1:**19
    amendments to, **2:**24–25,
        2:48–49
    defining, **2:**56
    early childhood education
        and, **5:**11–12
    objectives of, **2:**15
    problems addressed by,
        2:15–16

provisions of
(*See* Individualized
education programs;
Least restrictive
environment; Protection
in evaluation procedures)
specific learning disabilities
and, **9**:11–12
specific procedures of, **2**:16
See also Individuals
With Disabilities
Education Act
Educational settings
diverse, **1**:31–32
variations by state, **1**:32
See also Least restrictive
environment
Egel, A. L., **8**:30
Ekwall, E., **3**:38
Electronic travel aids,
4:55–56, **4**:64
Elementary and Secondary
Education Act (ESEA).
See No Child Left
Behind Act
Eligibility decisions, **1**:22,
3:14–15, **3**:78, **7**:9–10, **7**:55
Elliott, J., **4**:5
Emotional disturbance
academic characteristics of,
11:10–11
anxiety, **11**:18–22
behavior intervention plans,
11:15–16
behavioral characteristics of,
11:12–14
cognitive characteristics of,
11:9–10
communication characteristics
of, **11**:14
defining, **1**:16, **1**:41, **11**:7–9,
11:35–37, **11**:39–40
functional behavioral
assessment and, **11**:15–16

improving social interactions,
11:13–14
medical treatment for,
11:37–38
physical characteristics of,
11:11–12
psychosomatic, **11**:11
terms used to describe,
11:10 (tab)
See also Emotional
disturbance, teaching
students with
Emotional disturbance, teaching
students with
anxiety, **11**:18–22
behavior intervention plans,
11:17–26
disruptiveness, **11**:27–29
nonattention (distractibility),
11:29–30
school opposition/
noncompliance,
11:23 (tab)
social problems, **11**:27–33
task avoidance, **11**:31–33
temper tantrums, **11**:24–26
tips for school opposition/
noncompliance,
11:23 (tab)
tips for school phobia,
11:21 (tips)
tips for teachers of, **11**:18 (tab)
tips for temper tantrums,
11:25–26
tips for test-taking, **11**:22 (tab)
trends/issues influencing,
11:35–37
Emotional problems,
11:17, **11**:47
Employment, sheltered/
supported, **5**:25, **5**:56
Empowerment movement, **7**:47
Enhanced image devices,
7:36–37, **7**:60

Enrichment, **3:**10, **3:**78,
     13:23–24, **13:**28–36, **13:**53
Enright, B., **3:**21
Entwistle, D., **4:**5
Entwistle, N., **4:**5
Epidural hematomas, **8:**26, **8:**64
Epilepsy, **8:**23, **8:**64
Epilepsy Foundation
     of America, **8:**47
Epstein, A., **5:**16
Epstein, J. L.
Equal access, **2:**14,
     2:41 (tab), 45–46
Equal protection clause, **2:**7–8,
     2:53, **2:**55
ERIC Clearinghouse on
     Disabilities and Gifted
     Education, **1:**11
Erin, J. N., **7:**8
Error analysis, **3:**38, **3:**78
Errors
     assessment, **3:**62–63
     halo effect, **3:**62
     integration, **3:**48
     logical, **3:**62
     of central tendency, **3:**62
     of leniency, **3:**62
     persevcration, **3:**38, **3:**48
     rotation, **3:**48
     sensitivity, **3:**62
Errors of central tendency, **3:**62
Errors of leniency, **3:**62
Ethell, R. G., **4:**5
Evaluation
     defining, **4:**64
     formative, **4:**23, **4:**64
     language, **10:**44
     process, **1:**24
     program, **3:**16–17, **3:**80
     progress, **1:**24, **3:**80
     protection in procedures, **1:**13,
          1:42, **2:**21–23, **2:**56
     speech, **10:**44
     summative, **4:**23, **4:**65

Event recording,
     3:46, **3:**78
Exceptional students,
     defining, **1:**41
Exceptionality decisions,
     3:12, **3:**78–79
Exclusion, **2:**19 (fig),
     2:42 (tab), **2:**49–50
Expressive language, **10:**43

Face validity, **3:**57, **3:**79
Families/community agencies.
     See Community
     collaboration; Early
     intervention; Family
     involvement; Transition
     services
Family involvement, **5:**7
     adverse affects of disability
          on family, **5:**38
     affect of exceptionalities on
          families, **5:**35–37
     gifted student concerns,
          5:37–38
     home–school
          collaboration barriers,
          5:41 (tab)–42 (tab)
     home–school collaboration
          barriers, overcoming,
          5:39–40, **5:**42
     institutionalization *vs.* home
          care issues, **5:**38
     types of, **5:**39
     with communication
          disorders, **10:**30
FAPE (free and appropriate
     education), **2:**55
Fazzi, D. L., **7:**7, **7:**11
Feedback
     auditory, **7:**37
     corrective/supportive,
          4:46–47, **12:**37, **12:**43
     defining, **4:**21, **4:**64
     tactile, **7:**31

Fetal alcohol syndrome, **5**:10, **8**:14, **8**:64
Finger spelling, **7**:40, **7**:60
Flexible promotion, **13**:25
Flexible scheduling, **3**:71, **4**:54, **4**:64
Flexible settings, **3**:71, **4**:54, **4**:64
Fluency disorder, **10**:10, **10**:43
Forlenza-Bailey, A., **4**:5
Formal assessments, **3**:11
Formal interviews, **3**:30
Formal observations, **3**:27, **3**:29
Formal tests, **3**:27, **3**:79
Formative evaluation, **4**:23, **4**:64
Forster, G., **6**:53
Foster, R., **10**:27
Foster homes, **5**:31–32
Frederick L. v. Thomas, **2**:39 (tab)–40 (tab)
Free and appropriate education (FAPE), **2**:55
Frequency, **7**:20 (tab), **7**:60
Fristoe, M., **10**:26
Fuchs, D., **9**:17
Full inclusion, **6**:21
Functional academic assessment, **9**:19, **9**:57
Functional behavioral assessment, **9**:19, **9**:57, **11**:15–16, **11**:47
Functional hearing losses, **7**:24, **7**:25 (tab), **7**:60
Funding, **6**:15, **6**:16–17, **6**:44

Gallagher, J., **13**:11, **13**:19, **13**:20, **13**:45
Gallaudet Research Institute (GRI), **7**:22
Gallup, A. M., **11**:39
Gardner, H., **13**:43
Giangreco, M. F., **12**:59
Gickling, E., **3**:20
Giddan, J. J., **10**:27
Gifted, defining, **13**:53

Gifted and Talented Children's Education Act, **1**:33–34, **13**:10–11
Gifted and talented students
academic characteristics of, **13**:18–19
behavioral characteristics of, **13**:20–21
characteristics of, **13**:15–22, **13**:16 (tab)–17 (tab)
cognitive characteristics of, **13**:15–18
communication characteristics of, **13**:21–22
concerns of families with, **5**:37–38
creative ability, **1**:34, **1**:40
creative-productive giftedness, **13**:43
criteria other than intelligence test to determine, **13**:42–43
defining, **1**:16, **1**:41
evolving concept of giftedness, **13**:41–42
federal legislation concerning, **13**:9–11
identifying gifts/talents, **1**:35–36
identifying students as, **13**:12–14
intellectual ability of, **1**:34
leadership ability of, **1**:35
physical characteristics of, **13**:19–20
schoolhouse giftedness, **13**:43
specific academic ability, **1**:34–35
state definitions of, **13**:11–12
terms used to describe, **13**:10 (tab)
underrepresented groups in category of, **13**:44–45

visual/performing arts ability
of, **1**:35, **1**:40
See also Gifted and talented
students, teaching
Gifted and talented students,
teaching
acceleration tactics, **13**:36–40
acceleration/advancement
approach, **13**:25–27
criteria other than intelligence
test, **13**:42–43
enrichment approach,
13:23–24
enrichment tactics, **13**:28–36
extending knowledge in
content areas, **13**:31–33
extending knowledge into
new areas, **13**:33–36 (fig)
practicing/polishing skills,
13:28–31 (fig)
teacher tips, **13**:24 (tab),
13:45–46
trends/issues influencing,
13:41–46
Glaser, W., **4**:43
Goals 2000: The Educate
America Act, **6**:31, **6**:33
adult literacy/lifelong
learning, **6**:27–28
advocacy, **6**:12–13
applying to child with special
needs, **6**:30
mathematics/science, **6**:27
overview of, **6**:22, **6**:23
(tab)–**6**:24 (tab)
parental participation, **6**:29
safe/disciplined and
alcohol-/drug-free
schools, **6**:28–29
school completion, **6**:24–25
school readiness, **6**:22, **6**:24
standards, **6**:31, **6**:33
student achievement/
citizenship, **6**:25–26

teacher education/
professional
development, **6**:26–27
See also Individuals With
Disabilities Education
Act; No Child Left
Behind Act
Goldman, R., **10**:26
Good, T., **4**:13
Goss v. Lopez, **2**:39 (tab)
Grammar, **10**:44
Grand mal (tonic-clonic)
seizures, **8**:23, **8**:64
Gray Oral Reading Test–4, **3**:37
Greene, J. P., **6**:53
Greenwood, C., **3**:22, **4**:46
Greer, B. B., **8**:49
Greer, J. G., **8**:49
GRI (Gallaudet Research
Institute), **7**:22
Griffin, N. S., **13**:11
Grossman, H., **12**:24–25
Group data, **3**:50
Group homes, **5**:30–31, **5**:55
Group-administered
tests, **3**:27, **3**:79
Gruenewald, L., **12**:67
Guertin, T. L., **13**:45
Guide dogs, **4**:55

Hairston v. Drosick, **2**:39 (tab)
Hall, V., **4**:46
Halo effect errors, **3**:62
Haloed, **3**:56
Handicapped Children's
Early Education
Assistance Act, **5**:11
Handicapped Children's
Protection Act, **2**:48–49, **2**:55
Harcourt Educational
Measurement, **3**:37
Hard-of-hearing
defining, **7**:18–19, **7**:21, **7**:60
See also Hearing impairments

Hart, C. A., **8**:30

Haskins, R., **5**:15

Havertape, J., 3:20

Head Start, **5**:11, **5**:15,
  5:55, **6**:7, **6**:9

HeadSmart Schools program,
  8:27–28

Hearing acuity, **3**:40

Hearing aid, **4**:50–51, **4**:64, **7**:41
  troubleshooting, **7**:50–51

Hearing impairments
  academic characteristics of,
    7:23–24
  behavioral characteristics of,
    7:24–27
  central hearing losses, **7**:57
  cognitive characteristics of,
    7:22–23
  communication characteristics
    of, **7**:27–28 (tab)
  conductive hearing losses,
    7:19, **7**:56
  deaf culture and, **7**:26, **7**:59
  defining, **7**:6, **7**:18, **7**:60
  educational implications of,
    7:57–58
  ethnicity and, **7**:26
  functional hearing losses,
    7:24, **7**:25 (tab), **7**:60
  history of schools for deaf
    students, **7**:17–18
  integrating deaf/hearing
    students, **7**:26–27
  manual communication
    for, **7**:58
  measuring hearing loss,
    7:19–21
  mixed hearing losses, **7**:57
  oral communication for, **7**:58
  prevalence of, **7**:21–22, **7**:56
  senorineural losses, **7**:19,
    7:56–57
  signs of, **7**:28 (tab)
  teacher tips, **7**:28 (tab)
  technology for, **7**:58
  total communication for, **7**:58
  See also Deaf-and-blind/
    deaf-blind

Heart conditions, **8**:12, **8**:64

Hebbeler, K., **5**:24

Hematomas, **8**:26, **8**:64
  subdural, **8**:26, **8**:66

Hemophilia, **8**:13, **8**:59, **8**:64

Henderson, A. T., **5**:42 (tab)

*Hendrick Hudson District Board
  of Education v. Rowley,*
  2:41 (tab), **2**:45–46

Highly qualified teacher, **2**:31–32

Ho, A. S. P., **4**:5

Hobson v. Hansen, **2**:36 (tab)

Hodgkinson, H. L., 44

Holmes, D. L., **8**:29

Home-based programs,
  5:12–14, **5**:55

Homeless child/wards of
  court, **2**:34

Homework buddies, **9**:38–39

Honig v. Doe, **2**:19 (fig), **2**:42 (tab),
  2:49–50

Hospital-based programs,
  5:13–14, **5**:55

Humphries, T., **7**:26

Hunsaker, S. L., **1**:35–36

Hyperactivity-impulsivity,
  9:23–24, **9**:45 (tab), **9**:57

Hyperopia, **7**:9–10, **7**:60

IDEA. *See* Individuals With
  Disabilities Education Act

IDEIA. *See* Individuals With
  Disabilities Education
  Improvement Act

IEP. *See* Individualized
  education programs

IFSP (individualized family
  service plan), **2**:25, **2**:54,
  2:55, **12**:71

Imber-Black, E., **5**:42 (tab)

Immaturity, **3**:47
Immunodeficiency, **8**:12
Inattention, **9**:46–47, **9**:57
Incidental learning, **7**:14
In-class field trip, for math skills, **12**:42 (fig)
Inclusion, **1**:21–22, **1**:41, **6**:21, **6**:38–39
    as school reform, **6**:21, **6**:38–39
    defining, **6**:45
    full, **6**:21
    mainstreaming as, **2**:54, **2**:56, **5**:29–30, **5**:56
    of student with medical/ physical/multiple disabilities, **8**:56–59, **8**:57 (tab)
    of student with mental retardation, **12**:67–68
    technology role in, **6**:38–39
    See also Least restrictive environment
Independent living, **5**:23, **5**:30, **5**:32, **8**:31, **12**:31, **12**:55, **12**:58
Independent practice, **4**:40, **10**:36–37
Indirect (consultative) services, **1**:26, **1**:40, **1**:41, **5**:12, **5**:55
Individual data, **3**:50
Individual family service plan (IFSP), **5**:12, **5**:55, **12**:33
Individualized education programs (IEP), **1**:13, **1**:23–24, **2**:54, **8**:43
    amendments to, **2**:33
    decision-making process and, **2**:23–**2**:24
    defining, **1**:42, **2**:55, **3**:79
    due process hearing, **2**:21
    for student with communication disorder, **10**:41–42

for student with mental retardation, **12**:6–7, **12**:33, **12**:71
individualized family service plan, **2**:25, **2**:54, **2**:55, **12**:71
least restrictive environment requirement of, **2**:23
measurable goals requirement of, **2**:17, **2**:28
prior written notice requirement of, **2**:21
protection in evaluation procedures provision of, **2**:21
reasons for, **2**:17, **2**:20
sample of, **2**:18 (fig)–19 (fig)
team members required by, **2**:20 (fig)
Individualized family service plan (IFSP), **2**:25, **2**:54, **2**:55, **12**:71
Individualized transition plan (ITP), **2**:26, **2**:55–56, **5**:23, **5**:56, **12**:63, **12**:71
Individually administered tests, **3**:27
Individuals With Disabilities Education Act (IDEA), **2**:12 (tab), **2**:25–26, **2**:54
    assistive technologies under, **2**:26
    defining, **2**:56
    discrimination protection, **1**:13
    mandates of, **1**:12–13, **4**:54, **6**:37–38
    on educational settings, **1**:31–32
    on emotional disturbance, **11**:7–8, **11**:35–36
    on learning disabilities, **9**:7–8, **9**:9
    on mental retardation, **12**:9

on transition services, **5:**23
preschool services under,
　5:10–11 (fig)
See also Education for All
　Handicapped Children
　Act; Individuals With
　Disabilities Education
　Act (IDEA), amendments
　to; Individuals With
　Disabilities Education
　Improvement Act; Least
　restrictive environment
Individuals With Disabilities
　Education Act (IDEA),
　amendments to
discipline policies, **2:**28–29
individualized education
　program, **2:**28
manifestation
　determination, **2:**29
parental consent for
　reevaluation,
　2:12 (tab), **2:**27
preschoolers, **5:**12
streamlined reevaluation,
　2:27–28
Individuals With Disabilities
　Education Improvement Act
　(IDEIA), **2:**13, **2:**25–26, **2:**56
assessment language/
　communication mode,
　2:32–33
highly qualified teacher
　requirement, **2:**31–32
homeless child/wards of
　court, **2:**34
individualized education
　program provisions, **2:**33
learning disabled
　identification, **2:**32
special education students in
　general education, **2:**33
transition planning, **2:**33
Inference, **3:**61–62, **3:**79

Informal interviews, **3:**30, **3:**79
Informal observations,
　3:27, **3:**29, **3:**44
Informal tests, **3:**27, **3:**79
Institutions, for adults with
　special needs, **5:**33
Instruction
computer-assisted, **4:**5
defining, **4:**5, **4:**7, **4:**64
teaching as, **4:**5
See also Direct instruction,
　principles of; Instruction,
　adapting for students
　with special needs;
　Instruction, delivering;
　Instruction, evaluating;
　Instruction, managing;
　Instruction, planning
Instruction, adapting for
　students with special
　needs, **4:**31–38
ability training, **4:**39–40
behavior therapy, **4:**38
classwide peer tutoring, **4:**47
cognitive behavior
　modification,
　4:41, **4:**42 (fig)
cognitive skills training,
　4:41, **4:**43
cooperative learning, **4:**45–46
counseling therapy, **4:**43–45
critical thinking, **4:**43
direct instruction, **4:**40
learning strategies
　training, **4:**45
peer tutoring, **4:**46
peer-directed learning, **4:**46
precision teaching, **4:**39
social skills training, **4:**47–48
Instruction, delivering, **4:**17–23
adjusting instruction, **4:**21
　(tab), **4:**22–23
monitoring student learning,
　4:21 (tab)–22

motivating students, **4:**20
overview of, **4:**18 (tab)
presenting content, **4:**17–20
presenting lessons, **4:**17–19
providing relevant
    practice, **4:**20
teaching thinking skills,
    4:19–20
Instruction, evaluating, **4:**23–29
informing students of
    progress, **4:**27
maintaining student progress
    records, **4:**26 (fig)–27
making judgments about
    student performance,
    4:28 (fig)–29
monitoring engaged
    time, **4:**25
monitoring student
    understanding, **4:**23–25
overview of, **4:**24 (tab)
using data to make decisions,
    4:27–28
Instruction, managing, **4:**14–17
creating positive
    environment, **4:**16–17
overview of, **4:**15 (tab)
preparing for instruction,
    4:15–16
using time productively, **4:**16
Instruction, planning, **4:**7–14
actively involving
    students, **4:**14
analyzing groupings, **4:**10–11
analyzing task, **4:**10
assessing student skills, **4:**9
communicating realistic
    expectations, **4:**13–14
considering contextual
    variables, **4:**10
deciding how to teach,
    4:11–13
deciding what to teach,
    4:9–11

establishing gaps in actual/
    expected performance,
    4:11
establishing sequence, **4:**10
explicitly stating
    expectations, **4:**14
maintaining high
    standards, **4:**14
monitoring
    performance/replanning
    instruction, **4:**13
overview of, **4:**8 (tab)
pacing, **4:**13
selecting methods/materials,
    4:12–13
setting goals, **4:**12
Instructional adaptations, to
    increase communication/
    motility, **4:**49–50
amplification systems, **4:**51
braille, **4:**52, **7:**10, **7:**13, **7:**15,
    7:16, **7:**34, **7:**35 (tab)
calculators, **4:**53
canes, **4:**55
communication boards, **4:**50
computers, **4:**53–54
electronic travel aids,
    4:55–56
guide dogs, **4:**55
hearing aids, **4:**50–51
Kurzweil reading
    machines, **4:**53
optacons, **4:**52–53
prostheses, **4:**56–57
telecommunication devices,
    4:51–52
test modifications, **4:**54
wheelchairs, **4:**56
Instructional diagnosis,
    3:22, **3:**79
Instructional programs, keys to
    success in, **5:**47–50
commitment to normal life
    experiences, **5:**49

commitment to remedial
    programming, **5:**49
compatible physical
    environment, **5:**49
encouraging appropriate
    behavior, **5:**50
individualized planning,
    5:48–49
lifelong learning, **5:**50
Integration errors, **3:**48
Intellectual abilities, **1:**34, **1:**42,
    2:32, **3:**34–37, **9:**9
    intelligence interviews,
        3:36–37
    observing intelligence,
        3:34, 36
    overview of, **3:**35
        (tab)–36 (tab)
    testing intelligence, **3:**34
Intellectual functioning, **12:**71
Intelligence. *See* Intellectual
    abilities
International Baccalaureate
    (IB), **13:**26
Interval recording, **3:**45, **3:**79
Intervention assistance. *See*
    Prereferral interventions
Intervention assistance team
    (IAT), **3:**10, **3:**79
Interviews, **3:**26, **3:**30–31
    academic achievement,
        assessing, **3:**38–39
    formal, **3:**30
    informal, **3:**30, **3:**79
    intelligence, **3:**36–37
    language, **3:**44
    perceptual-motor, **3:**48
    psychological, **3:**46–47
    structured, **3:**30
    to assess academic
        achievement, **3:**38–39
    unstructured, **3:**30
Irrelevant activity,
    11:31, **11:**47

*Irving Independent School District
    v. Tatro,* **2:**42 (tab), **2:**46, **2:**54
ITP (individualized transition
    plan), **2:**26, **2:**55–56, **5:**23,
    5:56, **12:**63, **12:**71

Jackson, D. W., **7:**23, **7:**24, **7:**27,
    7:40, **7:**42
Jakob K. Javits Gifted and
    Talented Students Act, **13:**11
Jatho, J., **7:**26, **7:**42
Job coach, **5:**25, **5:**48, **5:**56, **12:**54
Johnson, D. W., **4:**45
Johnson, F., **12:**67
Johnson, N. E., **13:**45
Johnson, R. T., **4:**45
Jorgensen, J., **12:**67
Journals/articles (resources)
    assessment, **3:**92–93
    communication disorders,
        10:57–58
    emotional disturbance,
        11:60–63
    fundamentals of special
        education, **1:**54–55
    gifted and talented child,
        13:64
    learning disabilities, **9:**67–68
    legal foundations, **2:**66
    medical/physical/multiple
        disabilities, **8:**80–82
    mental retardation, **12:**84–85
    public policy/school
        reform, **6:**56
    sensory disabilities,
        7:77–79
    transitions, **5:**67
Juvenile rheumatoid arthritis,
    8:20, **8:**64

Kanner, Leo, **8:**29
Kember, D., **4:**5
Kentucky School System
    reform, **6:**34–35

Kevin T. v. Elmhurst Community School District No., **2:**44 (tab)
Key Points
  assessment, **3:**75–76
  communication disorders, **10:**42–43
  effective instruction, **4:**61–62
  emotional disturbance, **11:**43–46
  fundamentals, **1:**39–40
  gifted and talented child, **13:**51–52
  learning disabilities, **9:**55–56
  legal foundations, **2:**53–54
  medical/physical/multiple disabilities, **8:**61–62
  mental retardation, **12:**69–70
  public policy/school reform, **6:**43–44
  sensory disabilities, **7:**53–58
  transitions, **5:**53–54
Key Vocabulary
  assessment, **3:**76–81
  communication disorders, **10:**43–45
  effective instruction, **4:**62–66
  emotional disturbance, **11:**46–47
  families/community agencies, **5:**54–56
  fundamentals, **1:**40–43
  gifted and talented child, **13:**52–53
  learning disabilities, **9:**56–57
  legal foundations, **2:**54–56
  medical/physical/multiple disabilities, **8:**62–66
  mental retardation, **12:**70–72
  public policy/school reform, **6:**44–46
  sensory disabilities, **7:**59–62
Kirk, S. A., **9:**51
Klinefelter syndrome, **12:**14, **12:**71

Koestler, F., **7:**8
Koppitz, E. M., **3:**47
Kreimeyer, K. H., **7:**26
Kurzweil reading machines, **4:**53
Kwan, K. P., **4:**5

Lagomarcino, T., **5:**24
Lahey, B. B., **9:**44
Language development, **3:**43–44
  language test components, **3:**43
  using interviews, **3:**44
  using observations, **3:**44
Language disorders, **10:**44
Language evaluation, **10:**44
Larry P v. Riles, **2:**38 (tab)–39 (tab), **6:**10, **6:**45
Larsen, L. M., **13:**11
Larsen, M. D., **13:**11
Latency recording, **3:**46, **3:**80
Law, continuing changes in, **2:**7
Lead poisoning, **8:**11 (tab), **8:**64
Leadership ability, **1:**35, **1:**42, **13:**10, **13:**42
Learning centers,
  for reading, **9:**31
Learning disabilities (LDs)
  academic, **9:**51
  academic characteristics of, **9:**23
  assessing, **9:**17–19
  behavioral characteristics of, **9:**23–24
  category growth, **9:**12, **9:**14
  causes of, **9:**15–16
  cognitive characteristics of, **9:**22
  communication characteristics of, **9:**24–25
  criteria for identifying, **9:**8–9
  defining, **9:**7–8, **9:**49–50, **9:**57
  defining, variations by state, **9:**51–52
  developmental, **9:**51

discrepancy criterion removal, **9:**9
distribution of students with, by state, **9:**13 (tab)–**9:**14 (tab)
growth in specific learning disabilities category, **9:**11–12
physical characteristics of, **9:**23
prevalence of, **9:**11
subtypes of, **9:**51
transition of students with, **9:**52
See also Learning disabilities (LDs), improving classroom behavior for students with; Learning disabilities (LDs), teaching students with
Learning disabilities (LDs), improving classroom behavior for students with
daily reports, **9:**37 (fig)
homework buddies, **9:**38–39
study skills, **9:**37–39
work habits, **9:**35–37
Learning disabilities (LDs), teaching students with, **9:**25–41
general interventions, **9:**26 (tab)
math skills, **9:**32–33
reading skills, **9:**27–32
social relations, **9:**39–41
study skills, **9:**37–39
trends/issues influencing teaching of, **9:**49–52
work habits, **9:**35–37
written language skills, **9:**33–35
Learning strategies training, **4:**45, **4:**64

Least restrictive environment (LRE), **1:**13, **1:**27–28, **2:**23, **2:**41, **2:**54, **2:**56, **12:**61
defining, **5:**30, **5:**56, **12:**71
Ledesma, J., **4:**5
Lee, V. E., **5:**15
Leff, D., **7:**11, **7:**15
Legal fees, **2:**42 (tab), **2:**46–48
Legal foundations, of special education
balance perspective in, **2:**51–52
brief history of, **2:**9–10
early issues in, **2:**44–45
overview of important laws, **2:**10–11
overview of influential court cases, **2:**36 (tab)–44 (tab)
Supreme Court rulings, **2:**45–50
See also *individual laws and individual cases*
Legally blind, **7:**9, **7:**60
Legg-Calvé-Perthes disease, **8:**21, **8:**64
Lehr, C., **5:**18
Lehr, F., **9:**28
Lemon v. Bossier Parish School Board, **2:**38 (tab)
Leukemia, **8:**11 (tab), **8:**64
Leventhal, J. D., **7:**36
Levine, D. U., **4:**5–6
Levy, S. E., **8:**15
Lewis, R. B., **8:**56–58, **8:**57 (tab), **10:**18–20
Lieberman, L., **7:**29
Lifelong learning, **5:**50, **6:**27–28
Light v. Parkway School District, **2:**43 (tab)
Liles, C., **8:**15–16, **8:**43, **8:**55–56
Limb deficiencies, **8:**21–22, **8:**64
Listening-skills training, **7:**34, **7:**35 (tab)

Living arrangements, for adults
with special needs
alternative living unit, **5:**31
foster homes, **5:**31–32
group homes, **5:**30–31
independent living, **5:**32
institutions, **5:**33
Lloyd, J., **4:**40
Logical errors, **3:**62
Long, E., **12:**67
*Lora v. New York City Board of
Education,* **2:**40 (tab)–41 (tab)
Loudness, **7:**19–20, **7:**60
Louisiana Department of
Education, **13:**12
Low vision, **7:**60–61
Luckner, J., **7:**24, **7:**38,
7:42, **7:**50
Luetke-Stahlman, B.,
7:24, **7:**42, **7:**50
Lynch, E. W., **8:**56–58,
8:57 (tab)

Mainstreaming, **2:**54, **2:**56,
5:29–30, **5:**56
See also Least restrictive
environment
Mangrum, C. II, **5:**26
Manifestation determination,
2:29, **2:**56
Manual movements, **7:**40, **7:**61
Marburger, C. L., **5:**42 (tab)
Marder, C., **5:**24
Marland, S., **13:**41–42
Maryland State Department of
Education, **13:**11
Mastery, defining, **9:**32
Mathematics, improving,
6:27, **9:**32–33, **9:**34 (fig)
McBurnett, K., **9:**44
McKinney, J. D., **9:**51
McMeniman, M. M., **4:**5
Measures of process disorders,
9:18–19

Medical disabilities, **8:**9–16
AIDS, **8:**12–13
cystic fibrosis, **8:**12
fetal alcohol syndrome, **8:**14
heart conditions, **8:**12
hemophilia, **8:**13–14
identification by medical
symptoms, **8:**9–10
maternal cocaine use, **8:**14–15
medically fragile/technology
dependent groups,
8:15–16
other health impairments,
8:10–11 (tab)
prevalence of, **8:**10
special health problems,
8:14–15
Medical procedures, to ensure
appropriate education,
2:46, **2:**48, **2:**54
Medical treatment, for emotional
disturbance, **11:**37–38
Medically fragile, **8:**15, **8:**64
Medical/physical/multiple
disabilities
academic characteristics
of, **8:**38
behavioral characteristics of,
8:39–40
cognitive characteristics of,
8:37–38
communication characteristics
of, **8:**40–41
distribution of child with,
8:7–8 (fig)
home *vs.* institutional care for,
8:55–56
inclusion of student with, **8:**56
inclusion of student with,
overcoming barriers to,
8:56–59, **8:**57 (tab)
medical disabilities, **8:**9–16,
8:10–11 (tab)
multiple disabilities, **8:**33–35

physical characteristics of, **8:**39
physical disabilities, **8:**17–31,
    8:25 (tab)
relationship to federal
    disability categories,
    8:7 (fig)
See also Medical/
    physical/multiple
    disabilities, teaching
    students with
Medical/physical/multiple
    disabilities, teaching
    students with, **8:**43–53
adapting instruction, **8:**47–49
common adaptations, **8:**49–50
encouraging socialization, **8:**53
facilitating communication,
    8:50–52
fostering independence,
    8:52–53
general tips for, **8:**45 (tab)
identifying disabilities, **8:**44
key areas of assistance,
    8:46–47
questions to ask about, **8:**44,
    8:45 (tab)–**8:**46 (tab)
residual functioning, **8:**52–53
Mental retardation, **1:**16, **1:**42
academic characteristics
    of, **12:**30
as primary/secondary
    condition, **12:**28
behavioral characteristics
    of, **12:**31
characteristics of, **12:**2 (tab)
cognitive characteristics
    of, **12:**30
communication characteristics
    of, **12:**31–32
defining, **12:**6, **12:**9, **12:**71
genetic conditions as cause
    of, **12:**13–14
graduation rates of student
    with, **12:**63–64

health problems as cause
    of, **12:**15
inclusion of student with,
    12:67–68
individualized education
    program, **12:**6–7
learning environments for
    student with, **12:**67
mild/moderate/severe/
    profound retardation,
    12:10 (fig)–**12:**11 (tab)
physical characteristics of,
    12:30–31
prevalence of, **12:**11
preventing, **12:**62 (tab)
problems during pregnancy/
    birth as cause of, **12:**15
recent advances in
    treatment/services,
    12:65–67
self-determination
    and, **12:**64
transitioning from school to
    work, **12:**63–64
See also Mental retardation,
    diagnosing; Mental
    retardation, teaching
    students with
Mental retardation, diagnosing,
    12:17–25
adaptive behavior area,
    12:17, **12:**19–25
adaptive behavior, defining,
    12:21
adaptive behavior scales,
    12:21
adaptive skill areas evaluated,
    12:21 (tab)–23 (tab)
age-related criteria for,
    12:24–25
intellectual functioning
    area, **12:**17
Mental retardation, teaching
    students with, **12:**33–51

by making adaptations,
      12:33–34
family tips for, 12:34,
      12:36 (tab)
functional math skills,
      12:41–42 (fig)
functional reading skills,
      12:38–41 (fig),
      12:39 (fig), 12:40 (fig),
      12:41 (fig), 40 (fig)
functional writing, 12:40
general interventions for,
      12:37 (tab)
grading systems for,
      12:47–49
individualized education
      program, 12:33
individualized family services
      plan, 12:33
leisure skills, 12:50–51
school adaptive behavior,
      12:45–49
task analysis, 12:43–45
task completion, 12:38
teacher tips for,
      12:35 (tab)
trends/issues influencing,
      12:61–64
work skills, 12:49–50
See also Severe disabilities,
      teaching student with
Metropolitan Achievement
      Tests, 3:37
Meyer, C., 3:39
Meyer, L. H., 12:55
Michaud, L. J., 8:25, 8:26, 8:27
Mild/moderate/severe/
      profound retardation,
      12:10 (fig)–12:11 (tab)
Miller, L., 3:21
Minitests, 9:30 (fig), 9:57
Minnesota Standards for Services
      to Gifted and Talented
      Students, 13:12

Minnesota State Advisory
      Council for the Gifted and
      Talented, 13:12
Mizuko, M., 10:16
Mobility, 7:14, 7:61
Mobility aids, 7:34, 7:35 (tab)
Mock, D., 9:17
Molloy, D. E., 9:17–18
Moore, S. D., 1:35–36
Moores, D., 7:17, 7:21, 7:23,
      7:24–25, 7:26, 7:42
Moran, M., 6:41
Morgan, P. L., 9:17
Morphology, 10:10–11, 10:44
Mowat Sensor, 4:55–56
Muir, S., 7:38
Multiple disabilities, 8:34–35
Multiple intelligences,
      13:43, 13:53
Multiple or severe disabilities,
      1:16, 1:42
      See also Severe disabilities,
      teaching student with
Multiple sclerosis, 8:20–21
Murphy, D. S., 8:56–58, 8:57 (tab)
Muscular dystrophy,
      8:19–20, 8:65
Myelomeningocele, 8:24
Myopia, 7:9, 7:61

NAGC (National Association for
      Gifted Children), 13:25–27
Nania, P. A., 5:18
A Nation at Risk: The Imperative
      for Educational Reform,
      6:19–20
National Association for
      Gifted Children (NAGC),
      13:25–27
National Association
      of the Deaf, 7:42
National Autistic Society, 8:28
National Center for Education
      Statistics, 1:31, 5:9, 5:10

National Commission on
    Excellence in Education,
    6:19–20
National Council on Educational
    Standards and Testing,
    6:31–32
National Dissemination Center
    for Children with
    Disabilities (NICHY),
    11:44–46
National Education Goals,
    5:10, **6:**19–20, **6:**45
National Educational
    Standards and
    Improvement Council, **6:**31
National Governors'
    Association, **6:**20, **6:**34
National Head Injury
    Foundation (NHIF), **8:**27–28
National Information Center,
    10:38
National Institute on Deafness
    and Other Communication
    Disorders Information
    Clearinghouse, **7:**58
National Joint Committee on
    Learning Disabilities
    (NJCLD), **9:**15, **9:**50
National Research Council, **1:**13
Nechita, A., **1:**35
Needs assessments, **4:**41, **4:**64
Nephrosis/nephritis,
    8:11 (tab), **8:**65
Neurological disorders, **8:**22–25
    cerebral palsy, **8:**23–24
    epilepsy, **8:**23
    overview of, **8:**25 (tab)
    spina bifida, **8:**24
    spinal cord injury, **8:**24–25
Newland, T. E.,
    7:12–13, **7:**30
Newman, L., **5:**24
NHIF (National Head Injury
    Foundation), **8:**27–28

NICHY (National Dissemination
    Center for Children with
    Disabilities), **11:**44–46
NJCLD (National Joint
    Committee on Learning
    Disabilities), **9:**15, **9:**50
No Child Left Behind Act, **2:**12
    (tab), **2:**29–31, **2:**54, **6:**10,
    6:37–38, **6:**45
Nonattention (distractibility),
    11:29–30, **11:**47
Noncategorical, **12:**18, **12:**71
Noncompliance (oppositional
    behavior), **11:**22–24, **11:**47
Nonmanual movements,
    7:40, **7:**61
Nonphysical disruptions,
    11:27–28, **11:**47
Normal field of vision, **7:**9, **7:**61
Normalization, **12:**61, **12:**72
Normative peer comparisons,
    4:28, **4:**64
Norm-referenced tests, **3:**29, **3:**80,
    4:9, **4:**64
Norms, **3:**8–9, **3:**80
Nystagmus, **7:**10, **7:**61

Objective-referenced test. *See*
    Criterion-referenced tests
Observations, **3:**25–26, **3:**29–30
    active, **3:**29, **3:**77
    defining, **3:**80
    formal, **3:**29
    informal, **3:**27, **3:**29, **3:**44
    language, **3:**44
    of achievement, **3:**38
    of sensory acuity, **3:**40–41
    passive, **3:**29, **3:**80
    perceptual-motor, **3:**48
Occupational and
    social skills, **3:**42
OCR (Optical character
    recognition), **7:**36 (tab),
    7:38, **7:**61

Ocular motility, **7:**10, **7:**61
Oden, M., **13:**20, **13:**41, **13:**42
Office of Civil Rights, **6:**11, **6:**13
Office of Educational Research
    and Improvement, **13:**45,
    13:48, **13:**49
Office of Special
    Education Programs
    (OSEP), **6:**13–14, **6:**45
Ogbu, J. U., **13:**48
On Your Own
    assessment, **3:**89
    communication
        disorders, **10:**55
    effective instruction, **4:**73
    emotional disturbance,
        11:55–56
    families/community
        agencies, **5:**63
    fundamentals of special
        education, **1:**51
    gifted and talented child,
        13:61–62
    learning disabilities, **9:**65–66
    legal foundations of special
        education, **2:**63
    medical/physical/multiple
        disabilities, **8:**73–74
    mental retardation, **12:**79
    public policy/school
        reform, **6:**53
    sensory disabilities, **7:**69–71
Ooms, T., **5:**42 (tab)
Operant conditioning,
    4:38, **4:**65
Opportunity-to-learn (OTL)
    standards, **4:**46, **6:**12,
    6:33, **6:**45
Oppositional behavior
    (noncompliance),
    11:22–24, **11:**47
Optacons, **4:**52–53
Optical character recognition
    (OCR), **7:**36 (tab), **7:**38, **7:**61

Oral communication,
    for students with
        vision/hearing
        impairments,
        7:39–40, **7:**39 (tab)
Organizations (resources)
    assessment, **3:**93
    communication disorders,
        10:58–59
    effective instruction, **4:**77
    emotional disturbance,
        11:63–65
    fundamentals of special
        education, **1:**54–55
    gifted and talented child,
        13:65
    learning disabilities, **9:**68–69
    medical/physical/multiple
        disabilities, **8:**83–84
    mental retardation, **12:**86–87
    public policy/school reform,
        6:56–57
    sensory disabilities, **7:**79–85
    transitions, **5:**68
Orientation, **7:**14, **7:**61
Ornstein, A. C., **4:**5–6
Orr, A. L., **7:**7, **7:**11, **7:**13, **7:**14,
    7:15, **7:**34
Orr, S., **4:**5
Orthopedic impairments,
    8:17–18, **8:**65
    prevalence of, **8:**18
Orthopedic or other
    health impairments,
    1:16–17, **1:**42
Orthosis, **8:**52, **8:**65
Osborn, J., **9:**28
OSEP (Office of Special
    Education Programs),
    6:13–14, **6:**45
Osteogenesis imperfecta,
    8:20, **8:**65
Osteomyelitis, **8:**21, **8:**65
O'Sullivan, P. J., **5:**18

OTL (Opportunity-to-learn)
standards, **4:**46, **6:**12,
6:33, **6:**45
Outcomes-based accountability,
3:23, **6:**35

Pace, **4:**13, **4:**65
Panitch v. State of Wisconsin,
2:40 (tab)
Parental participation, **6:**29
Partially sighted, **7:**61
PASE v. Hannon, **2:**41 (tab)
Passive observation, **3:**29
Pathsounder, **4:**55
Paul, P. V., **7:**23, **7:**24,
7:27, **7:**40, **7:**42
Paulson, F., **3:**39
Paulson, P., **3:**39
Peavey, K. O., **7:**11, **7:**15
Peck, C. A., **12:**55
Peer tutoring, **4:**46–47, **4:**65
Peer tutoring, classwide,
4:47, **4:**63
Peer-directed learning, **4:**46
*Pennsylvania Association of
Retarded Citizens v.
Commonwealth of
Pennsylvania,* **12:**65–66
PEP (protection in evaluation
procedures), **1:**13, **1:**42,
2:21–23, **2:**56
Perceptual-motor development,
3:47–48
Perceptual-motor
interviews, **3:**48
Perceptual-motor
observations, **3:**48
Perceptual-motor tests,
3:47–48, **3:**80
Performance assessment,
3:24, **3:**80
Perret, Y. M., **8:**22, **8:**47
Perseveration errors,
3:38, **3:**48

Perspective
assessment, **3:**73–74
communication disorders,
10:35–38
effective instruction, **4:**59–60
emotional disturbance,
11:39–41
fundamentals, **1:**37–38
gifted and talented, **13:**47–49
learning disabilities, **9:**53–54
legal foundations, **2:**51–52
medical/physical/multiple
disabilities, **8:**55–59
mental retardation, **12:**65–68
public policy/school reform,
6:37–42
sensory disabilities, **7:**47–51
transitions, **5:**51–52
Petit mal seizures, **8:**23, **8:**65
Pfiffner, L. J., **9:**44
Phenylketonuria (PKU),
12:14, **12:**72
Phonetic cues, **9:**29, **9:**57
Phonology, **10:**10–11, **10:**44
Physical disabilities, **8:**17–31
autism, **8:**28–31
craniofacial anomalies, **8:**22
defining, **8:**65
juvenile rheumatoid
arthritis, **8:**20
Legg-Calvé-Perthes
disease, **8:**21
limb deficiencies, **8:**21–22
multiple sclerosis, **8:**20–21
muscular dystrophy, **8:**19–20
neurological disorders,
8:22–25
orthopedic impairments,
8:17–18
osteogenesis imperfecta, **8:**20
poliomyelitis, **8:**18–19
traumatic brain injury, **1:**17,
1:43, **8:**25–28, **8:**66
Physical disruptions, **11:**27, **11:**47

Pilmer, S. L., **8**:15
Pogrund, R. L., **7**:7, **7**:11
Poliomyelitis, **8**:18–19, **8**:65
Portfolios, **3**:26, **3**:39, **3**:80
Post-school interventions,
    5:50, **5**:56
Post-school transitions,
    5:23, **5**:24–25, **5**:37
Poteet, J., **3**:21
Powers, M. D., **8**:29, **8**:30
Pragmatics, **10**:11, **10**:44
Pratt, S., **8**:30
Precision teaching, **4**:39, **4**:65
Prereferral interventions
    defining, **1**:9, **1**:22, **1**:42, **3**:80
    determining eligibility, **1**:22
    evolution of, **1**:11–12
    growth in population
        receiving, **1**:19–20
    individualized
        education programs
        (*See* Individualized
        education programs)
    perspective on, **1**:37–38
    process evaluation, **1**:24
    purpose of, **3**:11
Preschool
    attendance increase, **5**:9–10
    early intervention during,
        5:9–10
    Individuals With Disabilities
        Education Act and,
        5:10–12, **5**:11 (fig)
    transition to K-12 education
        system, **5**:18–19
    Ypsilanti Perry Preschool
        Project, **5**:15–16
President's Commission on
    Excellence in Special
    Education, **1**:13
Private school, **2**:42 (tab),
    2:46–47, **2**:54
Process disorders,
    9:19, **9**:57

Program evaluation
    defining, **3**:80
    large-scale, **3**:16–17
    teacher's own, **3**:17
Programmed learning, **13**:37,
    13:39, **13**:53
Progress evaluation,
    1:24, **3**:80
Prostheses/prosthetic devices,
    4:56–57, **4**:65, **8**:65
Protection in evaluation
    procedures (PEP), **1**:13,
    1:42, **2**:21–23, **2**:56
Psychoeducational assessment,
    3:9, **3**:81
Psychological development,
    assessing, **3**:45–47
    personality tests, **3**:45
    psychological interviews,
        3:46–47
    psychological observations,
        3:45–46
Psychological interviews,
    3:46–47
Public Law 94–142. *See*
    Education for All
    Handicapped Children Act
Public policy
    impact on special education,
        6:39–40
    political effects on,
        6:10–11
    See also School reform
Pupil unit allocation method,
    6:16–17
Purcell, J. H., **13**:45

Quay, H., **3**:46

Rakes, T., **3**:21
Randomization without
    replacement, **4**:60
RAP mnemonic, **4**:45
Rapport, establishing, 60

Reading, improving
   analytical programs for,
      9:27, 9:56
   fostering motivation/interest,
      9:30–32
   reading comprehension,
      9:28–30
   sight word recognition, 9:28
   taped texts for, 9:6
   whole language programs for,
      9:27, 9:57
Reading Excellence Act, 6:20
Reading First, 2:30–31, 6:10, 6:20
Reality therapy, 4:43, 4:65
Reber, M., 8:30
Receptive language, 10:44
Redl, F., 4:44
Referral, 1:22, 1:42
   See also Prereferral
      interventions
Reflection
   assessment, 3:3–4, 3:85–87
   communication disorders,
      10:5, 10:51
   effective instruction, 4:4, 4:70
   emotional disturbance, 11:3–4,
      11:51–52
   families/community agencies,
      5:3–4, 5:59–60
   fundamentals of special
      education, 1:4, 1:48
   gifted and talented child,
      13:3–4, 13:57–58
   learning disabilities,
      9:3–4, 9:62
   legal foundations of special
      education, 2:4, 2:60
   medical/physical/multiple
      disabilities, 8:3, 8:69–70
   mental retardation, 12:3–4,
      12:75–76
   public policy/school reform,
      6:3, 6:49
   sensory disabilities, 7:3, 7:65

Regular education initiative
   (REI), 6:21, 6:45
Rehabilitation Act, 2:53, 9:44
Reichert, E. S., 13:45
Reis, S. M., 13:45
Related services,
      1:26, 5:12, 10:42
   as part of individualized
      education program,
      1:23, 11:45, 12:33
   defining, 1:42–43, 6:45
   growth in numbers receiving,
      1:19–20
   mandated, 1:31, 2:48, 6:40,
      8:17, 8:43, 12:9
Related services personnel,
      1:20, 3:12
Reliability, 3:50, 3:81
Reliability coefficient,
      3:50, 3:81
Remedial education, 3:10, 3:81
Renzulli, J., 13:18, 13:43
Representativeness, 3:50–51, 3:81
Residual functioning,
      8:52–53, 8:65
Resources
   assessment, 3:91–93
   communication disorders,
      10:57–59
   effective instruction, 4:75–77
   emotional disturbance,
      11:57–65
   families/community agencies,
      5:65–68
   fundamentals of special
      education, 1:53–55
   gifted and talented child,
      13:63–65
   learning disabilities, 9:67
   legal foundations of special
      education, 2:65–66
   medical/physical/multiple
      disabilities, 8:75–83
   mental retardation, 12:81–87

public policy/school reform,
    6:55–57
sensory disabilities, 7:73–85
Respondent conditioning,
    4:38, 4:65
Response to intervention (RTI),
    9:17, 9:18
Rheumatic fever,
    8:11 (tab), 8:65
Rogers, C., 4:44
Rogers, M., 4:49
Rogers, P. A., 7:7, 7:11,
    7:13, 7:14, 7:15, 7:34
Rose, L. C., 11:39
Rotation errors, 3:48
RTI (response to intervention),
    9:17, 9:18
Rubrics, 3:31
Rusch, F., 5:24
Ryser, G., 7:15

Saccuzzo, D. P., 13:45
Safe schools, 6:28–29
Samuelowicz, K., 4:5
Schaller, J., 7:15
Schattman, R., 12:59
Schnur, E., 5:15
School reform, 6:19–35
    Goals 2000 (See Goals 2000:
        The Educate America
        Act)
    impact on special
        education, 6:35
    inclusion as, 6:21, 6:38–39
    national goals, 6:19–20
    national standards, 6:30–33
    opportunity-to-learn
        standards, 4:46, 6:12,
        6:33, 6:45
    regular education
        initiative/inclusion, 6:21
    school restructuring,
        6:33–34, 6:45
    See also Public policy
School restructuring,
    6:33–34, 6:45
School-based enterprises,
    5:46, 5:56
Schoolhouse giftedness,
    13:43, 13:53
Schrier, E. M., 7:36
Schumaker, J., 4:45
Schweinhart, L., 5:16
Screening, 3:7–8
    defining, 3:81
    early, 3:8–9
    late, 3:9–10
    tests for, 3:28
    See also Protection in
        evaluation procedures
Section 504 of the Rehabilitation
    Act, 2:11 (tab), 2:13, 2:14–15,
    2:56, 4:54
Seizures
    grand mal (tonic-clonic), 8:23,
        8:64
    petit mal, 8:23, 8:65
Self-Assessment/Answer Key
    assessment, 3:1–3,
        3:83–85, 3:87
    communication disorders,
        10:1–5, 10:47–51, 10:53–54
    effective instruction, 4:1–3,
        4:67–69, 4:71
    emotional disturbance, 11:1–3,
        11:49–51, 11:53
    families/community agencies,
        5:1–3, 5:57–59, 5:61
    fundamentals of
        special education,
        1:1–4, 1:45–47, 1:49
    gifted and talented child,
        13:1–3, 13:55–57, 13:59
    learning disabilities, 9:1–3,
        9:59–61, 9:63
    legal foundations of
        special education,
        2:1, 2:57–60, 2:61

medical/physical/multiple
disabilities, **8:**1–3,
8:67–69, **8:**71
mental retardation, **12:**1–3,
12:73–75, **12:**77
public policy/school reform,
6:1, **6:**47–49, **6:**51
sensory disabilities, **7:**1–3,
7:63–65, **7:**67
Self-care, **12:**47, **12:**57
Self-contained class, **4:**28, **4:**65
Self-determination, **12:**64, **12:**72
Self-direction, **12:**46–47
Self-help skills, **3:**42
Semantics, **10:**11, **10:**44
Sensitivity errors, **3:**62
Sensorineural hearing loss,
7:19, **7:**61
Sensory acuity, assessing,
3:39–**3:**41 (fig)
Sensory disabilities, teaching
student with
assistive listening, **7:**41
collaboration role in, **7:**52
communication system,
7:41–42
cued speech, **7:**40–41
eliminating barriers overview,
7:34–38, **7:**35 (tab)–36
(tab), **7:**39 (tab)
empowering student, **7:**47–48
fostering independence,
7:42–45
future of, **7:**52
improving communication
overview, **7:**39 (tab)
oral communication, **7:**39–40
positive interaction tips,
7:44–45
sign systems, **7:**40
supporting accommodations
for, **7:**49–51
technology to eliminate
barriers, **7:**34, **7:**36–38

telecommunication
devices, **7:**41
total communication, **7:**40
understanding characteristics
specific to, **7:**49
See also Deaf-and-blind/
deaf-blind; Hearing
impairments; Visual
impairments
Sentner, S. M., **4:**5
Severe disabilities, teaching
student with, **12:**53–59
communication
considerations, **12:**56–57
community living and,
12:57–58
curriculum considerations,
12:56
defining severe disabilities,
12:54–55
instructional approaches,
12:58–59
mobility, **12:**57
prevalence of, **12:**55
self-care and, **12:**57
Shape distortions, **3:**48
Sheltered/supported
employment, **5:**25, **5:**56
Shin, H., **6:**33
Siblings, effect of
exceptionalities on, **5:**36–37
Sickle-cell anemia, **8:**11 (tab),
8:66
Sigafoos, J., **7:**26
Sign language, **7:**39 (tab), **7:**40
Silverman, L. K., **13:**44
Singleton, P., **7:**47
Site-based management,
6:34, **6:**35, **6:**46
Six-hour retarded child, 41
Skilled examiner, **3:**59–61
Skinner, D., **4:**5
Skull fractures, **8:**26, **8:**66
Smith, J., 14–15

Smith v. Robinson, **2:**42 (tab),
   2:47–49
Snellen Wall Chart, **3:**40
Social interactions, improving
   for student with emotional
      disturbance, **11:**13–14
   for student with learning
      disabilities, **9:**39–41
   Social problems, **11:**17, **11:**47
   Social skills, **7:**15
   occupational skills and, **3:**42
   school adaptive behavior and,
      12:45–46
   training in, **4:**47–48, **4:**65,
      12:45–46
Social values, affect on special
   education, **6:**8–10
Software
   math, **12:**41
   sight word recognition, **9:**28
Sonicguide, **4:**56
Spastic cerebral palsy, **8:**23–24
Special education
   categories of, **1:**15–17
   current reforms in, **6:**40 (*See
      also* Public policy; School
      reform)
   defining, **1:**43
   future of, **6:**41
   social values and, **6:**8–10
   See also Special education,
      economic factors driving
Special education, economic
   factors driving, **6:**13–17
   allocation methods, **6:**16–17
   federal review of state
      plans, **6:**14
   funding competition, **6:**15
   OSEP programs, **6:**13–14
   research priorities, **6:**15
Special education process. *See*
   Prereferral interventions
Special educators, continuing
   demand for, **1:**20

Specific learning disabilities
   defining, **1:**17, **1:**43
   See also Learning disabilities
Spectrum disorder, **8:**29
Speece, D., **9:**17–18
Speech disorders, **10:**44
   articulation disorder, **10:**9–10
   fluency disorder, **10:**10
   voice disorder, **10:**10
Speech evaluation, **10:**44
Speech or language
   impairments, **1:**17, **1:**43
Speech-language pathologist,
   10:17–18, **10:**39–41, **10:**44
Spina bifida, **8:**24, **8:**66
Spinal cord injuries, **8:**24–25, **8:**66
Spooner, F., **12:**43
Stahl, S. A., **9:**28
Standard behavior chart,
   4:39, **4:**65
Standards
   defining, **6:**31, **6:**46
   legislation on, **6:**37–38
   national, **6:**30–33
   opportunity-to-learn, **4:**46,
      6:12, **6:**33, **6:**45
Stark, J., **10:**27
Stem, B., **12:**43
Stereotypes, **3:**56, **3:**81
Stern, B., **12:**43
Stern, J., **6:**13
Sternberg, R. J., **13:**43
Strabismus, **7:**10, **7:**61
Strichart, S. S., **5:**26
Structured interview, **3:**30
Stuart, M., **7:**29
Student progress records,
   4:26 (fig)–27
Stuttering. *See* Fluency disorder
Subdural hematomas, **8:**26, **8:**66
Summative evaluation, **4:**23, **4:**65
Supported employment,
   5:25, **5:**56
Swan, M., **13:**33

Syntax, **10**:10–11
Synthetic speech devices,
   7:37, **7**:62

TA (transactional analysis),
   4:44, **4**:65
Talented, defining, **13**:53
TASH (The Association for
   Persons with Severe
   Handicaps), **12**:55
Task analysis, **3**:22, **3**:81, **4**:10,
   4:40, **4**:65, **12**:43–45, **12**:72
Task avoidance, **11**:31–33, **11**:47
Task Force on DSM-IV, **9**:45 (tab)
Taylor, R. L., **3**:7
Teacher
   egalitarian, **4**:59–60
   highly qualified, **2**:31–32
   humanitarian, **4**:60
   radomizer, **4**:60
Teacher education/professional
   development, **6**:26–27
Teacher training, reform in, **6**:40
Teacher unit allocation
   method, **6**:16
Teaching
   defining, **4**:5, **4**:7, **4**:66
   precision, **4**:39
   principles for effective, **4**:5–6
   tips for, **6**:42
Technical career programs,
   5:45–46
Technology, to increase
   communication/motility,
   4:53–54
Technology dependent,
   8:15–16, **8**:66
Tech-prep programs,
   5:45–46, **5**:56
Telecommunication
   devices, **4**:51–52, **4**:66,
   7:39 (tab), **7**:41, **7**:42
Temper tantrums, **11**:47
Terman, L., **13**:20, **13**:41, **13**:42

Test, D. W., **12**:43
Test modifications, **4**:54
Testing/tests
   achievement, **3**:37, **3**:77
   criterion-referenced, **3**:28–29,
      3:77–78, **4**:9, **4**:64
   defining, **3**:25, **3**:81
   diagnostic, **3**:28, **3**:78
   formal, **3**:27, **3**:79
   group-administered,
      3:27, **3**:79
   group/individual tests, **3**:27
   informal measures, **3**:27
   norm-/criterion-referenced
      tests, **3**:28–29
   norm-referenced, **3**:29, **3**:80,
      4:9, **4**:64
   screening/diagnostics, **3**:28
   test content, **3**:29
   test development, **3**:52–54
   test fairness, **3**:55–56
   test formats, **3**:27–28
   test modifications, **4**:54
The Association for Persons
   with Severe Handicaps
   (TASH), **12**:55
Thematic units, **9**:57
Thinking skills, **4**:19–20
Thomas, D., **5**:15
Thurlow, M. L., **3**:71,
   5:18, **6**:9, **6**:33
Thurlow, M. L., Wiley, H. I.,
   & Bielinski, J., **6**:60
Time sampling recording,
   3:46, **3**:81
Timothy W. v. Rochester,
   New Hampshire,
   School District, **2**:5–6,
   2:42 (tab)–43 (tab)
Tinker v. Des Moines Independent
   Community School District,
   2:36 (tab)–37 (tab)
Tonic-clonic (grand mal)
   seizures, **8**:23, **8**:64

Total communication, for student with vision/hearing impairments, **7**:39 (tab), **7**:40

Transactional analysis (TA), **4**:44, **4**:65

Transition plans, **5**:17–18
individualized, **2**:26, **2**:55–56, **5**:23, **5**:56, **12**:63, **12**:71

Transition services, **2**:26, **2**:33, **2**:56, **5**:6
defining, **5**:23, **5**:56
See also Community collaboration

Transitions
effect on families, **5**:36–37
See also Transition plans; Transition services; Transitions, types of

Transitions, types of, **5**:17–23
continued education, **5**:26–27
dropping out, **5**:20–23, **5**:21 (tab)
during school, **5**:19
employment/financial independence, **5**:24–25
everyday, **5**:19
post-school, **5**:23, **5**:24–25, **5**:37
preschool to K-12 education system, **5**:18–19
within general education classrooms, **5**:20

Traumatic brain injury (TBI), **1**:17, **1**:43, **8**:17, **8**:25–28, **8**:66

Tuberculosis, **8**:11 (tab), **8**:66

20/20 vision, **7**:8

Udvari-Solner, A., **12**:67

Unified system, **6**:35, **6**:46

Unstructured interview, **3**:30

U.S. Congress, **2**:16

U.S. Department of Education, **1**:11, **1**:15, **1**:19–20, **7**:10, **7**:11, **7**:21, **7**:30, **7**:56–58, **8**:6, **8**:29, **8**:34, **9**:14 (tab), **12**:11, **12**:61

U.S. Office of Civil Rights, **6**:46

Uslan, M. M., **7**:36

Validity, **3**:51–54, **3**:81

VanDeventer, P., **12**:67

Visual acuity, **3**:40, **7**:8, **7**:62

Visual functioning, **7**:10

Visual impairments, **1**:16, **1**:40
academic/cognitive characteristics of, **7**:11–14, **7**:54–55
appropriate literacy medium, **7**:16
behavioral characteristics of, **7**:14–15
brief history of special education and, **7**:7
communication characteristics of, **7**:15–16
defining, **7**:6, **7**:8, **7**:9, **7**:62
eligibility for students with, **7**:9–10, **7**:55
environmental modifications for, **7**:13
focusing difficulties, **7**:9–10
physical characteristics of, **7**:14
prevalence of, **7**:10–11, **7**:54
signs of, **7**:12 (tab)
teaching modifications for, **7**:13–14
teaching tips, **7**:16 (tab)
technological aid for, **7**:13
visual functioning, **7**:10

Vocabulary, defining, **10**:45

Voice disorder, **10**:10, **10**:45

Wagner, M., **5**:22, **5**:24

Walker, H. M., **3**:46

Walker, R., **6**:34

Wang, M. C., **4**:31–32

Ward, M., **4**:53

Wards of court/homeless child, **2**:34

Warner, M., **4**:45
Washington v. Davis, **2**:39 (tab)
Watson v. City of Cambridge,
    Mass., **2**:36 (tab)
Web sites (resources)
    effective instruction, **4**:75
    sensory disabilities, **7**:73
Weber, J., **11**:36
Wehman, P., **5**:44–45
Weikart, D., **5**:16
Weiss, J. A., **5**:18
Wheelchairs, **4**:56
Whole language program,
    9:27, **9**:57
Whorton, D., **4**:46
Wiederholt, L., **3**:37
Withdrawal, **3**:47, **11**:6, **11**:13
Wittrock, M. C., **4**:12
Work portfolios, **3**:31
Work-sample assessment,
    3:26, **3**:81
Written expression, improving
    checklists, **9**:33–34

defining, **10**:45
familiar words, **9**:34–35
focus on quantity, **9**:33
self-evaluation, **9**:34
software, **9**:35
timed exercises, **9**:35
Wyatt v. Stickney,
    2:38 (tab)

Yell, M. L., **2**:19 (fig), **2**:29,
    2:49–50
Yost, D. S., **4**:5
Young, C .L., **9**:17
Youth apprenticeships
    programs, **5**:45, **5**:56
Ypsilanti Perry Preschool
    Project, **5**:15–16
Ysseldyke, J. E., **3**:14,
    3:23, **3**:71, **4**:5, **5**:18,
    6:9, **6**:33, **12**:62

Zobrest v. Catalina Foothills
    School District, **2**:43 (tab)